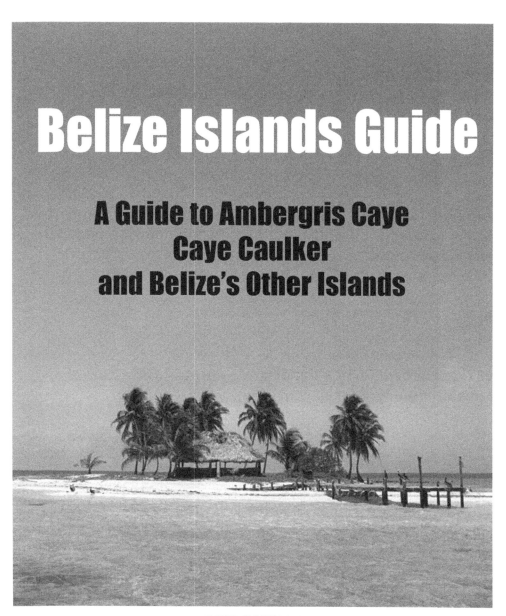

Belize Islands Guide

A Guide to Ambergris Caye
Caye Caulker
and Belize's Other Islands

LAN SLUDER

Belize Islands Guide
A Guide to Ambergris Caye, Caye Caulker
and Belize's Other Islands

Published by Equator Publications, Asheville, NC

Text and book design © copyright 2002-2010 by Lan Sluder. All rights reserved. Photos by Lan Sluder and Rose Lambert-Sluder. Cover and frontispiece photo and photos on page 29 and 62 by Tom Boyd, used by permission. Maps by Robert O'Hair.

ISBN: 978-0-9670488-6-4

EQUATOR Publications, Asheville
287 Beaverdam Road • Candler, NC 28715 USA
e-mail: lansluder@gmail.com • www.belizefirst.com

TABLE OF CONTENTS

Welcome to Ambergris Caye
And the Islands of Belize

By **LAN SLUDER**

Want a comfortable, shorts-and-sandals seaside vacation, at a moderate price? Just a bit off the beaten path but not too far, where the seafood is fresh and the beer is cold? Where the tap water won't make you sick?

An island with most of the modcons without the plastic tackiness, with decent diving, excellent snorkeling, beautiful water and pretty fair beaches? Where local folks are friendly and *hablan* English, though they may speak Spanish at home? A spot with dependably beautiful weather most of the time?

Then you'll enjoy Ambergris Caye or one of Belize's other beautiful islands.

Though it's developing fast, San Pedro, the only real town on Ambergris Caye, still remains mostly laidback and low-rise. Some of the streets have been paved with concrete cobblestones (alas!), but the side streets are still sand, and away from the main part of town the dirt roads are more paths than

A beach on North Ambergris Caye

streets. Golf carts are still the main form of transportation, albeit the number of cars on the island continues to rise, and in some areas of downtown the traffic is really bad. The air strip, despite being lengthened, is still a strip, not a port, and it's literally next door to town.

 No, this is not an undiscovered paradise. Yes, tourism is the number one industry in what was once a fishing village. Well over one-half of the 240,000 or so international travelers to Belize each year end up here. Commercial fishing is now so far back in second place that you can't even see the hooks. This is not, however, the bloated tourism of Cancun, with millions of package tourists hitting the beach and sucking beer.

True, condos, houses and hotels are going up right and left. Development continues at a rapid pace south of town. North Ambergris, separated from the south by a river channel, and with a new bridge for golf carts, bikes and pedestrians spanning it, is starting to achieve critical mass, with electrical power even to once remote houses and hotels and rumors, or worse, of big resorts and casinos. Some even think there will be a road and bridge from the Mexican side. Still, most buildings on the island aren't higher than a tall coco palm, or three stories.

Hotels inexorably are getting more upmarket, with freshwater pools and aircon. Prices continue to go up, too, with the best suites in the best hotels going for the previously unthinkable - US$400 a day, and higher. But most hotels on Ambergris Caye are moderate by Caribbean standards. And a few rooms are available for US$25 or less. Have you checked what beachfront hotels in St. Thomas or Anguilla are getting these days? Or even in Cozumel?

This is not an island for backpackers looking for the cheapest deals by the sea. Neither is it for shoppers (though you can while away a few hours in San Pedro's gift shops), golfers (though there's a course on an island next door), gamblers (though there's a little bit of gaming), oenophiles (though there are two wine shops now, several restaurants have decent if small wine lists, and one restaurant makes and sells passable wines from imported grape juice), gourmandizers (though several island restaurants will satisfy even sophisticated palates and many serve dependably delicious meals), or those panting after one of those all-inclusive hedoheat experiences made famous in Jamaica (though the first *Temptation Island* reality show was shot on Ambergris Caye).

Ambergris Caye is not for those seeking the ultimate beautiful beach, or totally unspoiled diving, nor is it for sophisticates who summer in the Hamptons and winter in St. Barts. Yet, for both visitors and residents, the island continues to become more cosmopolitan. Restaurants are getting better. Expats from all over the world now call San Pedro home. The island is by far the first choice of Americans, Canadians and Europeans for their *pied de mer.* A number of Belize's most successful business people maintain vacation homes here.

In short, Ambergris Caye is at that very special point in the development of a tropical paradise. It is beyond boredom, a bit before mass discovery and just this side of just right. Shouldn't you pay a visit and take a look soon?

This new guide also covers Caye Caulker and the other beautiful islands of Belize.

Part of Barrier Reef Drive in San Pedro

PRACTICAL INFORMATION FOR YOUR TRIP

About Belize: Belize (known as British Honduras from 1862 to 1973) is on the Caribbean Coast of Central America, bordered by Mexico to the north and Guatemala to the west and south. To the east is the Caribbean Sea. In Belize waters are as many as 400 islands, most unpopulated specks of sand or mangrove. Belize is about the size of the state of Massachusetts — 8,866 square miles — with a population of about 333,000, about as many people as in metro Savannah, Georgia, making it one of least densely populated countries in the hemisphere. From north to south Belize is less than 200 miles in length, and at its widest point it is less than 70 miles across. Ambergris Caye is in Northern Belize, separated from Mexico's Yucatán by only a narrow channel of water. In fact, at some point in the geological past it was a stalactite hanging from the ceiling of the Yucatán. The island is about 25 miles long and 1 to 4 miles wide.

Ambergris: No, you won't find any whale vomit on the island. The waxy secretion of sperm whales, prized for use in perfumes, is sometimes found floating in tropical seas, but there is no convincing evidence that its presence on Ambergris Caye was the source of the name. (Some amateur historians say it was, however.) Locally, the island's name is pronounced Am-BURR-griss. Caye is pronounced key. Spanish speakers usually refer to a key as *cayo,* but one way it is not pronounced is kay.

Banks: Retail banks on the island include **Belize Bank, Alliance Bank, First Caribbean International** and **Atlantic Bank,** all on Barrier Reef Drive. **Scotia Bank** is across from Tropic Air on Coconut Drive. **Caye Bank,** on Coconut Drive south of town, is an international (offshore) bank and cannot do retail banking in Belize. Belize and Alliance banks are in new buildings, and Atlantic Bank has a new office, too. Belize Bank, ScotiaBank and Atlantic Bank have ATM machines that accept foreign-issued ATM cards. You will be charged a small fee, around US$2 by the bank, plus your home bank may also charge a fee. You will get funds in Belize dollars. Cash advances with Visa or MasterCard bank cards also are available on the island. There is a small fee, usually around US$5, for the cash advance, in addition to whatever fee or interest your bank card issuer may charge. If you are stuck in San Pedro without funds, friends or family can wire money to you via a bank or Western Union.

Bargaining: In general, prices in Belize stores and shops are fixed, and there is no bargaining. Of course, bargaining is an accepted practice for big-ticket items such as real estate. For better prices at hotels, you may want to do some low-key bargaining, especially in the off-season. Just say that you're on a budget and ask if any discounts are available. Ask: "Are there any discounts now?" or "Is there a better rate?" Walk-in rates can be up to one-third off the prevailing rack rate, especially from late August to early November. You may also get a discounted rate by booking direct via the internet rather than through a travel agency. Tour guides or dive shops might offer a better rate for groups or repeat business.

Bugs: Surprise! Mosquitoes, sandflies (no-see-ums) and other noxious bugs are not as big a problem on the island as you might think. San Pedro Town sprays for mosquitoes. Only on North Ambergris and the far south of the island, mostly away from the beach and the prevailing sea breezes, are mosquitoes a threat. Truth to say, though, the mosquito level varies from year to year -- after rainy periods outside of town they can be bothersome. There are sandflies in some areas of the island, especially on North Ambergris, but they don't even begin to match the sandfly quotient around Hopkins or in South Carolina.

Business Hours: Most businesses open around 8 a.m. and close at 5 or 6 p.m. A few close for lunch, usually from 1 to 2 p.m. Gift shops, groceries and some other shops are open in the evening until 8 or 9 p.m. and also are open on weekends and many holidays.

Cars/Golf Carts: Although there are privately owned cars and trucks on the island (a permit from the San Pedro town council is required before you can bring a vehicle in by barge), rental cars are not available on Ambergris Caye. Golf carts are available from several companies on the island. Cart rentals cost nearly as much as a car rental: around US$40 for an 8-hour rental, US$50 to $65 for a 24-hour day, and about US$250 for a week's rental. Discounts may be available off-season or for longer-term rentals. Among the cart rental companies on the island are **Cholo's, Moncho's, Castle Cars, Ultimate Golf Carts** and **Island Adventures.** Both electric and gas carts are available – if you're doing a lot of driving, you'll want to get a gas cart. Valid driver licenses from your home country are required to rent and operate carts. Most hotels can arrange cart rental for you. For long-term stays, you can purchase a golf cart for US$2,000 and up. Keep in mind that maintenance and upkeep on carts can be expensive. Replacing batteries can cost you several hundred dollars.

Cell Phones: In addition to an older analog system, **Belize Telecommunications, Ltd.** now offers "Digicell," a digital service on the GSM 1900 Mhz technology. As with cell phone serv-ice nearly everywhere, cell plans in Belize are complex, but BTL offers a package for US$50 a month that includes 200 minutes, and a US$75 a month plan that includes 400 minutes. Generally, you can figure on paying at least US25 cents a minute for cell service. You can also purchase pre-paid cell service at a higher minute rate. Visitors to Belize can bring their GSM 1900 cell phone and buy a SIM card for around US$25. You can also rent a Digicell phone from BTL (at the office across the parking lot at the International Airport) for US$5 a day (not including usage). **SmartNet** is a digital cell service that began operating in 2005. Smart and BTL also have cellular internet service that start at around US$50 a month.

Children: **Kids are welcome at nearly all resorts on Ambergris Caye.** Children of all ages will have fun on the island, as long as their idea of fun isn't limited to malls and fast food restaurants. A hotel with a swimming pool is a must for many families traveling with kids. Most hotels can arrange baby-sitting. It's generally safe for older children to explore the island on their own, but they need to be warned about watching out for fast-moving cars on the island's narrow streets. Note that restaurants and bars on the island often are lax about enforcing the drinking age of 18, and some young teens seize the opportunity to try booze while on vacation. Drugs are pres-ent on the island, and your teenager may well be approached by dealers selling grass, or harder drugs.

Churches: The majority of Belizeans are Catholic, and the largest church on the island is the **San Pedro Roman Catholic Church** on Barrier Reef Drive. It has masses in English and Spanish. Another Catholic church in the San Pablo residential area was damaged by Hurricane Keith in 2000 and currently is closed. Several other religious denominations also are repre-sented on the island. Among the churches are **Assembly of God Church, San Pedro Baptist Church** and **Living Word Church.**   Check with your hotel for times and places of servic-es. On the mainland are many Catholic and Protestant churches, along with one mosque. There is no temple but Jews meet in local homes in Belize City.

Climate: Ambergris Caye, like most of Belize, has a sub-tropical climate. Frosts and freezes are unknown. **Weather in San Pedro is similar to that in South Florida,** with temps ranging from the upper 50s F on the rare cool winter day to above 90 on a hot summer day. From November through March, expect lows in the low to mid 60s and highs in the low to mid 80s. The rest of the year, expect lows in the low 70s and highs in the high 80s to low 90s. Prevailing winds off the water keep beach and shore areas pleasant most of the time. Winds sometimes go calm in summer, especially in August and September. Occasionally during the late fall and winter "Northers" blow in, chilling the air and kicking up winds. Ambergris Caye gets about 55 inches of rain a year, about the same as Atlanta. July through November normally is the rainiest time on the island, but even during this "rainy season" it is unusual to have long rainy periods, and sunny weather returns after a day or two. Humidity is high, peaking in the summer at above 80%.   Most hotels on the island have air-conditioning.

Credit Cards: **Most hotels, restaurants and shops accept credit cards,** typically **MasterCard** and **Visa** and sometimes **American Express. Discover** is not widely accepted. Surcharges of up to 5% on credit card use are becoming less common but are still applied by a few businesses – ask before using your card.

Crime: **Most visitors to Ambergris Caye feel entirely safe.** However, crime does exist on the island, as "rich tourists" are a magnet for bad elements from other parts of Belize or from other parts of Central America. The island has seen several murders in recent years, and burglaries of homes and condos are unfortunately common. Crack cocaine and other drugs are present on the island. Use common sense, avoid walking in unlit or isolated areas at night, including dark areas of beach, and keep an eye on cameras and other personal possessions. Leave all your fancy jewelry and Rolex watches at home. They will impress only thieves. Several high-profile resort property owners in San Pedro and elsewhere on the islands reputedly have connections with organized crime and narco money laundering. Ask around, and you'll soon find out who they are and which hotels and resorts they own.

Dining: **Ambergris Caye has by far the widest and best choice of restaurants in Belize.** The range is enormous, from street vendors who sell tacos for 50 U.S. cents to simple burger and pizza places, to seafront restaurants where trendy lobster or shrimp dishes go for US$30 or more and an icy mojito or martini will set you back ten or twelve bucks. In general, restaurant prices in San Pedro are about the same as in a resort area of the U.S., such as Florida. *(See the Dining sections below for more information on restaurants.)*

Dress: **Belize is a casual place, and San Pedro is even more casual than the rest of the country.** You don't need evening clothes or a coat and tie or other U.S.-style business dress. You'll live in tee-shirts and shorts. A really dressy occasion for men might require a guayabera or collared short-sleeve shirt and khakis, and for women a casual resort dress.

Drink: The "national drinks" of Belize are **Belikin** beer and, some say, red or orange **Fanta.** Belikin, mostly widely sold by the 9 1/2 oz. bottle with a Maya temple at Altun Ha on the front, is a tasty light-bodied beer. Expect to pay about US$2 to $3 a bottle in bars for regular Belikin (a premium or export version in a larger bottle is more expensive.) **Bowen & Bowen** has a virtual monopoly on beer and soft drinks in Belize, brewing Belikin, including a **Belikin Stout,** plus **Lighthouse** lager. It also produces **Guinness Stout** under license. Because of Bowen's legal monopoly, excellent and cheaper beers from Mexico and Guatemala are generally not available in Belize. Red Stripe and Heineken from Caricom countries, but prices are higher than Belikin. In groceries, a 12 oz. can of **Bud** or **Miller** – one can – may go for US$4 or $5. Bowen also is the **Coca-**

Cola bottler in Belize, bottling various Coke products including Fanta. **Coke Light,** similar to Diet Coke, is now widely available in Belize. Belizean rum, in either white or gold varieties, is excellent and cheap. **One Barrel** is among the best brands, and **Caribbean** is poured in many bars. In groceries, a good local rum runs about US$8 to $14 a bottle, and in bars and restaurants local rum drinks are usually about US$2 or $3, one-third or one-half the cost of drinks with imported liquor. Belize-made vodka and gin are available, but they're pretty awful. The legal drinking age in Belize is 18; this rule often isn't enforced.

Drugs: Despite its reputation as a source of marijuana and, more recently, as a transshipment point for cocaine and other drugs from South America, Belize has strict laws on the sale and use of illegal drugs, with prison terms and fines for offenders. Some visitors to San Pedro are approached by locals offering drugs, and if you are, remember that Hattieville Prison is not where you would want to spend a vacation. Anytime you buy drugs from strangers, you are taking a risk. Not a few Belizeans smoke marijuana, some fairly openly, but if you are caught smoking breeze your vacation could be spoiled – you could spend quality time with the police, you might get a fine and possibly a quick departure from the country, or worse. Belize is not Jamaica or The Netherlands.

Electricity: **Current is 110 volts AC/60 cycles, same as in the U.S., and plugs/outlets are the same, too.** Electricity on the island, mostly provided from Mexico by **Belize Electricity Limited (BEL),** is at least twice as expensive as in the U.S., so air conditioning and power-hungry appliances are a bit of a luxury; some budget hotels may charge extra for A/C rooms. Most parts of the island, except the far north and south-ern tip, are now on the power grid. Service is generally depend-able, though there are frequent power surges and some out-ages. BEL is working to expand service to most of the island.

Embassies: The **U.S. Embassy** formerly was in Belize City in a historic building that was originally constructed in New England in 1866 and later dismantled and shipped to what was then British Honduras. The embassy was relocated in 2007 to a new US$50 million compound in Belmopan. Vinai Thummalapally, a college roommate of Barack Obama, is the U.S. Ambassador to Belize.   Contact the U.S. Embassy at 501-227-7161. The web site is www.belize.usembassy.gov. Canada, the U.K., Mexico, Guatemala, Costa Rica, Taiwan and about a dozen other countries have ambassadors or other representatives either in Belize City or Belmopan.

Entry & Customs: **All visitors to Belize, including children, must have a valid passport,** good for at least six months beyond departure date (this rule about the date may not always be imposed). Most visitors, including those from the U.S., the U.K., EU, Australia, New Zealand and Canada and about 60 other countries, do not need visas. *(See the Belize Tourism Board web site at www.travelbelize.org for information on visas.)* Entry for international visitors arriving in Belize by air is at **Philip Goldson International Airport** in Ladyville, 9 miles north of Belize City. Immigration officials grant stays of up to 30 days. To get the longest period, say you plan to stay "about a month." Tourist stays may be extended by paying a fee of US$25 per month for up to six months, then US$50 a month for an additional six months, but you will need to apply for extensions at immigration offices. You will go through customs at the International Airport, usually a quick and fairly painless process. Note: You cannot bring a firearm to Belize, even if it is licensed in your home country. If you are flying to San Pedro from the International Airport (a 20-minute flight on Maya Island Air or Tropic Air), proceed to the domestic terminals. If you are going into Belize City, either to catch a water taxi or to depart from the **Municipal Airport,** get a taxi at the front of the airport. The fixed rate is US$25 (BZ$50) into Belize City. *(For more information, see Getting to San Pedro section below.)*

Exit Fees and Prohibited Exports: Leaving Belize by international air, you pay a US$39.25 exit fee/tax. Most airlines except American include this fee in your ticket price. If leaving by land to Mexico or Guatemala, or by sea, you pay a US$18.75 exit fee. You cannot export objects made of coral, turtle shell or snakeskin. You also cannot take out orchids, fruits or other flora without an export phytosanitary certificate.

Fitness Clubs and Gyms: **Fitness equipment** is available at two places on the island, **Oscar's Gym,** and at the **San Pedro Fitness Club** near the south end of the airstrip, and also at some hotels. The Fitness Club (tel. 501-226-2683 gym, 226-2682 pool & tennis courts, www.sanpedrofitness.com) has a fully equipped air-conditioned gym, two competition-size lighted tennis courts, a 180,000-gallon fresh water pool and a bar and grill. It is open daily except for a few local holidays.

Gay and Lesbian Travelers: Belize does not have a high-profile gay and lesbian scene. There are no openly gay bars or clubs. However, Belizeans generally are easy-going about sexual matters — Belize welcomed a gay cruise ship visit when it was turned away from the Cayman Islands — and gay and lesbian travelers experience few difficulties. San Pedro is probably the best bet for gays, but it's definitely not Key West.

Golf: Ambergris Caye has no golf course, except a small mini-golf operation, but a water taxi away is **Caye Chapel Island Resort** with its stunning 18-hole, par-72 seaside course. Beautiful it is; cheap it is not. The cost of a day (9 a.m-4 p.m.) package is US$150 per person which includes unlimited golf, cart, clubs, use of the swimming pool, hot tub and private beach area. This does not include transportation to the island – US$20 per person round-trip by water taxi. For information: tel. 800-901-8938 or 501-226-8250, fax 226-8201; e-mail golf@cayechapel.com.

Government: Belize is a democratic member of the British Commonwealth. It has a Westminster-style system with a prime minister, an elected house of representatives and an appointed senate. The current prime minister is **Dean Barrow,** a U.S.-educated lawyer. He heads the **United Democratic Party**

(UDP), which came into office again in 2008. The opposition party is the **People's United Party (PUP).** Both parties are generally centrist. Politics in Belize is a freewheeling affair and often intensely personal. Belize has strong ties with the United States and Britain, but it also has cultivated ties with Taiwan, Cuba, Japan and other countries, often out of the need to seek foreign aid or development funding. In contrast with most countries in the region, Belize has a stable and thriving democracy. Typically, 70% or more of elegible voters go the polls. The next national elections will be held in 2013, unless called earlier by the UDP. Locally, San Pedro is governed by an elected town council.

Groceries: There are a number of small groceries on the island. The largest are **San Pedro Supermarket** at the north end of town, **Richie's** (across the street from San Pedro Supermarket) and **Island Supermarket** south of town. Island Supermarket is the largest and fanciest of the three but usually the most expensive. Other small groceries are located around the island, including **Marina's** south of town. **Super Buy** on Back Street is where many locals shop. These and other shops each have approximately the inventory of a large convenience store in the U.S., plus items such as frozen meats. In addition, there are small stores that specialize in meats. A good local bakery is **Casa Pan Dulce** (formerly La Popular). Fruits and vegetables can be purchased from street vendors or at small specialty shops. Costs for most food items, especially imported items, are considerably higher than in the U.S., often twice as high. Belikin beer can be ordered by the case from the Belikin distributor just south of town, near the Island Supermarket. However, even by the case beer in Belize isn't cheap – you'll pay about a U.S. dollar a bottle, but that's still a savings over supermarket prices. Liquor is sold in grocery stores – imported brands cost about twice U.S. prices, with local rum usually under US$10 a fifth. There are two wine shops on the island, **Wine DeVine,** on Tarpon Street near the airstrip, and **Premium Wines & Spirits** (a branch of a Belize City store) next to Fido's on Barrier Reef Drive. You'll generally pay twice U.S. prices for most wines. **Lagniappe Provisioning** (www.lagniappe-belize.com) will buy and deliver groceries, liquors and wines to you at your hotel, rental house or chartered boat, for a little over the prices you'll pay at supermarkets. **Caye Coffee** roasts and sells good Guatemalan coffees.

Handicap Access: Physically limited travelers will find very few handicap-accessible facilities anywhere in Belize, including Ambergris Caye. Rarely do hotels have rooms or facilities for those with limited mobility. On Ambergris Caye, a few hotels, including the SunBreeze, offer handicap-accessible rooms. In addition, sandy beaches, rough roads, old houses, small boats and rugged terrain may pose difficulties. That being said, most Belizeans are hospitable and helpful to everyone, and people with severe physical restrictions have traveled successfully in Belize. Check with your hotel in advance to see what type of facilities are available.

Health: **Standards of health and hygiene on Ambergris Caye are high, similar to that of popular resort islands in the Caribbean.** Not many visitors become ill from traveler's diseases or from drinking the water. While **malaria, dengue fever** and other tropical diseases are present in Belize, they are rare in San Pedro, and as a practical matter most visitors to Ambergris Caye don't get any special shots or take other precautions before they come. No shots are required for entry into Belize, except for yellow fever if you are coming from an infected area, such as parts of Africa or South America. However, it's always a good idea to keep tetanus-diphtheria, Hep A and B and other vaccinations up to date. Malaria prophylaxsis may be advised for extensive mainland travel; it is highly advised if you are going to remote mainland areas in southern Belize or into Guatemala. Chloroquine, taken once a week, starting two weeks before arrival, is usually all you need in most of the region. Better be safe than sorry. Check with the **U.S. Centers for Disease Control,** tel. 404-332-4559 or visit www.cdc.gov, for the latest information. The biggest vacation-spoiler on Ambergris is probably **sunburn.** You're only 18 degrees of latitude north of the Equator, and the sub-tropical sun is much stronger than back home.

Hotels: Ambergris Caye has about 100 hotels with about 1,800 rooms. Most are small, with 10 to 30 rooms. Only a few properties have more than 50 units, and none has as many as 100. You can choose from a variety of different kinds of properties – full-service beach resorts, condotels, cabaña colonies, budget hotels, and collections of beach houses. Prices start at around US$15-$25 a night and go about as far north as your pocketbook can stand. In addition, the island has dozens of vacation rental homes. *(See the Accommodations sections below for more information.)*

National Holidays: The following are legal public holidays in Belize:
New Year's Day - January 1
Baron Bliss Day - March 9 (date may vary)
Good Friday
Holy Saturday
Easter Sunday
Easter Monday
Labour Day - May 1
Commonwealth Day - May 24
St. George's Caye Day - September 10
Independence Day - September 21
Pan American Day (formerly Columbus Day) - October 12
Garifuna Settlement Day - November 19
Christmas Day - December 25
Boxing Day - December 26

In addition, on Ambergris Caye June 29 is the feast day of St. Peter, patron saint of the island. In recent years, the feast day has turned into a three-day festival. Among celebrations on *Dia de San Pedro* are blessings of boats.

Hurricanes: June through November technically is hurricane season in the Western Caribbean, but the September through early November period is the most likely time for tropical storms and hurricanes. About 85% of the hurricanes to hit Belize have arrived during the months of September and October. During the last half of the 20th century, only five hurricanes struck Belize, with the worst being Hattie in 1961. However, with the new millennium has come an increase in storm activity. Hurricane Keith hit Ambergris Caye in late September 2000, killing four and doing some US$150 million in damage, mainly on the back side of the island. In 2001, Tropical Storm Chantal threatened Ambergris but mainly caused a little beach erosion. Hurricane Iris in early October 2001 devastated the Placencia peninsula and rural Toledo District in southern Belize, killing 21, but caused no damage on Ambergris Caye. In August 2007, Hurricane Dean sideswiped Northern Belize on its way through the Mexican Yucatán, damaging crops and knocking down trees, but otherwise sparing most of Belize, including Ambergris Caye and Caye Caulker. Here is some data on hurricanes and tropical storms in Belize:

Number of storms making landfall in Belize since 1889:
In the past 120 years since weather records in Belize were formally maintained, Belize has seen the following storms make landfall:
21 hurricanes — average of 1 hurricane every 5 1/2 years
31 tropical storms – average of 1 tropical storm every 3 3/4 years
52 total hurricanes and tropical storms – average of 1 hurricane/storm every 2 1/4 years

Of the 21 hurricanes:
9 or 43% were in September
8 or 38% were in October
2 or 10% were in July
1 or 5% was in November
1 or 5% was in August
0 or 0% were in June

Of the 52 total hurricanes and tropical storms:

19 or 37% were in September
14 or 27% were in October7 or 13% were in June
5 or 10% were in August
4 or 8% were in July
3 or 6% were in November

Odds of a hurricane:
Odds of a hurricane in Belize in a given year: 17%
Odds of a hurricane in Florida in a given year: 68%
Odds of a hurricane on the U.S. Gulf Coast in a given year:67%
Odds of a hurricane on the U.S. East Coast in a given year: 47%

Most powerful storms to hit Belize:
• Unnamed hurricane, September 9, 1931, Belize City and Northern Cayes, 110 mph, estimated 2,500-3,000 deaths
• Hurricane Janet, September 28, 1955, Northern Belize, 165 mph, 16 deaths in Belize
• Hurricane Hattie, October 31, 1961, Belize City, 140 mph, estimated 225-310 deaths in Belize
• Hurricane Carmen, September 2, 1974,   skirted Northern Belize, 120 mph
• Hurricane Mitch, October 27, 1998, skirted Belize to the south, 155 mph
• Hurricane Keith, October 1, 2000, Ambergris Caye, 120 mph, 4 deaths in Belize
• Hurricane Iris, October 9, 2001, Placencia & Southern Belize, 145 mph, 21 deaths in Belize
• Hurricane Dean, August 20, 2007, Corozal District, Northern Belize, winds over 120 mph, no deaths, damage to some agricultural crops

Source: Belize National Meteorological Service, NOAA and other weather records

Internet: Internet access in Belize has been greatly improved over the past few years. **Belize Telemedia, Ltd.** now offers **DSL** in most of the country, for either PC or Mac. However, costs are much higher than in the U.S. or most other countries. Rates range from US$50 a month for 128 kbps to US$150 for 512kbps to US$250 for 2 Mbps. These are download rates, and in practice you may not get these speeds. In addition, there is an installation charge of US$100 (US$500 deposit for non-residents) and a monthly

HURRICANE DEAN IN AUGUST 2007
SPARES MOST OF BELIZE

Hurricane Dean, with winds of 165 mph, a powerful Category 5 storm, came ashore early in the morning of Tuesday, August 21, 2007, about 40 miles northeast of Chetumal, Mexico, near the cruise ship port of Costa Maya. It spared most of Belize, including San Pedro, Caye Caulker, Belize City, Belmopan, Cayo and all of southern Belize. No storm-related deaths were reported in Belize. Many trees were blown down in the Corozal Town area and elsewhere in Corozal District, and some buildings were damaged, but overall the impact was light. Ambergris Caye and Caye Caulker reported only tropical storm and perhaps some Category 1 winds, with little damage except that some older piers were destroyed and several homes had roof damage. In Belize City, Belmopan, San Ignacio, Dangriga, Placencia and Punta Gorda, residents reported only moderate rain and light, cooling breezes, with virtually no damage. In most areas, internet service was never disrupted. International and domestic flights resumed within a couple of days of the storm.

Agriculture in Northern Belize took the brunt of the storm. Up to 80% of Northern Belize's mature papaya plantings were flattened by winds (even tropical force winds can knock down papaya plants). One of northern Belize's major employers, Fruta Bomba, lost most of its papaya crop. Some of the sugar cane crop was damaged. There also was damage to corn, soy-beans, avocado and other crops. The rice industry was not affected. The total dollar damage is in the tens of millions of US dollars.

Hotels reported little if any damage, and nearly all either remained open or reopened within a few days of the storm. Most hotels on Ambergris Caye reported that they suffered no damage. A few had minor damage, downed trees and some limited beach erosion. Hotels on Caye Caulker and remote offshore cayes uniformly reported no damage, and most stayed open. Properties in Belize, Cayo, Stann Creek and Toledo districts uniformly report-ed no damage and remained open for business, except for those already closed for routine seasonal maintenance. The bottom line is that the tourism industry in Belize suffered very little damage.

modem rental fee of US$15 (or you can buy a modem for around US$155.) DSL from BTL is currently available in San Pedro, and also in Belize City, Caye Caulker, Belmopan, San Ignacio, Benque Viejo, Corozal Town, Punta Gorda and Placencia. **Dial-up** accounts are also available from BTL.

Connection speed is slow, usually 28 to 52 kbps. Dial-up internet service starts at around US$20 a month. Smart, a competing telcom in Belize, is now offering wireless DSL in many areas. Internet via digital **cable** is available in Belize City for around US$50 a month. Some residents use **satellite** internet, mainly from Hughes (formerly Direcway). Belize has many **internet cafés,** including **CyberCoffee** in San Pedro. Many hotels in San Pedro offer internet access for their guests, either wireless (sometimes free) or on a hotel computer.

Language: English is the official language of Belize, and it is spoken by nearly everyone on Ambergris Caye as a first, second or third language. Many native San Pedranos speak **Spanish** at home or among themselves. **Creole,** a combination of mostly English vocabulary with West African grammar, syntax and word endings, is used by many Belizeans of all backgrounds, but more so on the mainland than in San Pedro. Also on the mainland, **Garifuna** and **Maya** languages are spoken, and some Mennonites speak a **German** dialect. As many as two-thirds of Belizeans are bi- or trilingual.

Laundry: Many hotels do laundry for their guests, at rates lower than in the U.S. A small bag of dirty clothes washed, dried and folded is around US$5 depending on the hotel. San Pedro has several laundries including **Nellie's** (tel. 501-226-2454) on Pescador Drive. **Candise's Laundry** is next to Premium Wines & Spirits on Barrier Reef Drive. Expect to pay about US$6 to $7 for a 10-pound load, including washing and line drying. If your hotel doesn't provide laundry, Nellie's offers free pickup and delivery. Some hotels can also provide irons and ironing boards, if you absolutely have to press your pants. Nellie's also does ironing by request. There is no dry cleaner on the island. Local ladies may also be glad to earn a little extra money by doing laundry – just ask at your hotel or in residential neighborhoods where you see laundry hung out to dry.

Mail: The **San Pedro post office** (tel. 501-226-2250) is located on Barrier Reef. Hours are Monday-Friday 8—4:30. Mail service between Ambergris Caye and the U.S. is usually reliable but may take 10 days or longer. Mail service between Belize City and the U.S. is fast and reliable, rarely taking more than a week. The Belize Postal Service also now has an international express mail service. For fast, dependable but very expensive international express delivery, try **DHL Worldwide Express,** which has an office in Belize City (38 New Rd., tel. 501-223-4350.) **FedEx** has a service desk at the Tropic Air cargo office in San Pedro.

Maps: The best maps to San Pedro and Belize are listed below. Typical U.S. prices are as shown:

• *Belize Traveller's Map,* ITMB. The best general map to Belize, updated in 2005. US$8.95—$11.95.

• *Ambergris Caye, British Ordnance Survey Topographical Map,* 1:50,000-scale. Not up-to-date. US$14 (folded).

• *Driver's Guide to Beautiful Belize,* by Emory King. This mile-by-mile guide to most roads in Belize (but it does not cover the cayes) is really handy if you are traveling around the mainland. It's a 40-some page booklet in 8 1/2" x 11" format, updated annually, last in 2007 due to the death of Emory King. US$10—$14.

Several on-line maps of Ambergris Caye are available on www.ambergriscaye.com. Also **Google Earth** (earth.google.com) has moderately high resolution (about 200 meters) maps of San Pedro and part of North Ambergris Caye.

Media: The island has two weekly newspapers. The *San Pedro Sun* (tel. 501-226-2070, www.sanpedrosun.net) is operated by an expat couple, Ron and Tamarra Sniffin, from the U.S. *Ambergris Today* (tel. 501-226-3462, www.ambergristoday.com) is run by Dorian Nuñez.   An on-line news summary, the *San Pedro Daily*, is put together by Jesse Cope and posted on www.belizenews.com. National newspapers, including *Amandala,*

The Reporter, The Guardian (the UDP organ) and the *Belize Times* (the PUP paper), all weeklies published in Belize City, also are distributed in San Pedro. Cable TV, with some 50 channels from the U.S. and Mexico, is available on much of the island; it includes a channel devoted to events of interest to tourists and local residents. Several mainland TV stations, including Channel 5 and Channel 7, may also be picked up in San Pedro. *Belize First Magazine* (www.belizefirst.com) provides an updated news roundup of Belize and Caribbean news, and it maintains an archive of news items about Belize dating from 1997 to the present, the only such on-line archive available.

Medical: There is now a clinic on the island and several physicians, nurses and other medical professionals. The **San Pedro Polyclinic II** (501-226-2536) was established in great part due to the long-time efforts of the San Pedro Lions Club. In 2005, the year the new clinic opened, the San Pedro club was named the Lions Club of the Year, selected from more than 46,000 clubs in 193 countries.

Other medical services on the island:
Ambergris Hopes Clinic – 501-226-2660
Rene Hegar, DDS – 501-226-4595
Hyperbaric Chamber – 501-226-2851
Lions Health Clinic – 501-226-4052
Los Pinos Clinic — 501-226-2686
Lerida Rodriguez, MD — 501-226-2197
Otto Rodriguez, MD – 501-226-2854
San Pedro Chiropractic Clinic — 501-226-4695
Island Ferry Emergency--501-226-3232, Ch. 11 marine radio

A small offshore medical school, **Medical University of the Americas,** had a campus at the south end of the island. However, it closed.

Belize City is the center for medical care in Belize. Many serious problems can be treated at **Karl Heusner Memorial Hospital** in Belize City (Princess Margaret Dr., tel. 501-223-1548), a

modern public hospital albeit one plagued by equipment problems and supply shortages. It's hard to beat the rates, though
– under US$30 per day for a hospital room. There are seven
other public hospitals in Belize, including two regional hospitals:
the **Southern Regional Hospital** in Dangriga, and the
Northern Regional Hospital in Orange Walk Town.
Altogether, there are about 600 public hospital beds in Belize.

The public hospitals provide the four basic medical specialties:
internal medicine, surgery, pediatrics and OB-GYN. Karl
Heusner Memorial also provides neuro, ENT, physiotherapy,
orthopedic surgery and several other services. The quality of
these hospitals varies considerably. Karl Heusner Memorial —
named after a prominent Belize City physician — opened in
1997 and has much modern equipment, such as a CAT-scan,
though some Belizeans and expats complain that even this hospital is chronically short of supplies, including at times hygiene
supplies. In 2004-2005, it added new facilities including ones
for neurosurgery and trauma care. The Southern Regional
Hospital in Dangriga, which opened in 2000, is another modern
facility, with much of the same medical technologies and equipment as you'd find in a community hospital in an American
town.   However, other hospitals leave a lot to be desired. The
hospital in Orange Walk, for example, though it is being upgraded, still looks more like a refugee camp than a hospital, with
low concrete block buildings and limited equipment.

In addition to these public hospitals and clinics, Belize has three
private hospitals — **La Loma Luz,** a not-for-profit Seventh Day
Adventist hospital in Santa Elena near San Ignacio, and
Universal Health Services (which has merged in to Karl
Heusner Memorial) and **Belize Medical Associates,** two for-
profit facilities in Belize City.   Altogether these hospitals have
fewer than 60 hospital beds. There also are a number of physicians and dentists in private practice, mostly in Belize
City.

Government figures show Belize has fewer than one physician

per 1,000 population, or about 250 practicing physicians for a population of nearly 333,000, less one-half the rate in the U.S. Belize has about 500 nurses. Most physicians and dentists in Belize are trained in the U.S., Guatemala, Mexico or Great Britain. There are three so-called offshore medical schools in Belize (one each in Corozal Town, Belize City and Belmopan), but their graduates are unlikely to practice in Belize. A nursing school, affiliated with the **University of Belize,** trains nurses for work in Belize.

Those with even more serious or life-threatening problems may want to get care in Mexico, Guatemala or the U.S. A helicopter service, **Astrum Helicopters,** near Belize City (501-222-9462), can handle medevac.

The **Belize Disaster and Rescue Reponse Team** responds to injuries and accidents on Ambergris Caye. The **Island Ferry** is the focal point for the rescue team. Island Ferry captains have been trained in first aid and CPR. The rescue team offers ambulance service by boat for patients needing to go to Belize City.

Money: **The Belizean dollar traditionally has been exchanged at the rate of 2 Belize dollars to 1 U.S. dollar.** At banks, there is a small exchange fee and you will get slightly less than 2 Belize to 1 U.S. Money changers in border areas (not on Ambergris Caye) exchange money at a floating rate; usually it is higher than 2 to 1, up to about 2.1 to 2.2 Belize to 1 U.S., depending on current demand for U.S. dollars. However, most visitors will not be affected by any of this, and **there is no need to exchange U.S. dollars as these are still accepted virtually everywhere in Belize at a rate of 2 to 1.** You will probably get change in Belize dollars, or in a mix of Belize and U.S. currency. Common Belize paper-money denominations are the 100-, 50-, 20-, 10-, 5- and 2-dollar bills. Belize coins come in 1-dollar, 50, 25, 10, 5 and 1 Belizean-cent units. The 25-cent piece is called a shilling. Canadian dollars and European currencies are not commonly accepted on the island, and it may be difficult to change them on the island even at a bank. The Belize Bank branch at Goldson International Airport offers currency exchange seven days a week.

Nude Beaches: Belize's traditions are British, not Continental, so there are no clothing-optional beaches on the island. However, in privately owned or remote areas nude sunbathing has probably happened a time or two. Some female visitors, mainly Europeans, do go topless at hotel pools or beaches. Thongs or other brief swimsuits should not be worn in town.

Pharmacies: There are drug stores on the island and also many in Belize City. Many prescription drugs cost less in Belize than in the U.S., though pharmacies do not stock a wide selection of drugs. Ask your hotel for the nearest pharmacy. In general, in Belize prescriptions are not needed for antibiotics and many other drugs which may require prescriptions in the U.S., although pharmacies owned by physicians (common in Belize) may suggest a consultation with the doctor. It is a good idea to bring with you any prescription medicines you regularly need, as they may not be readily available in San Pedro or elsewhere in Belize.

Population: The 2000 Belize Census put Ambergris Caye's population at 4,499, up from 1,842 in the 1991 Census. San Pedro's official growth rate of 144% in the 1990s was the fastest of any major area in Belize. By mid-2009, the Belize Central Statistical Office put the island's population at 12,900. Counting tourists and temporary workers, at any one time now there can be more than 20,000 people on the island. Caye Caulker has an official population of around 1,400, but with the influx of people looking for work, the actual population may be larger. The entire country of Belize has a population near 333,000.

Sports: Just about any sea and warm-weather sport is available on or around Ambergris Caye. Snorkeling is world-class, though shore snorkeling is limited. **Diving** on the barrier reef is good and that around the atolls farther out is some of the best in the Caribbean. **Fishing,** whether flats fishing inside the reef or for bigger fish outside the reef, is excellent. You can **jet ski, parasail, windsurf, kitesurf, kayak, fly in an ultralight** and, on occasion, go **sky diving**. Candidly, sea **swimming** is only so-so, due to the amount of seagrass and, in some areas, the shallowness of the water near shore, but the water is effortlessly clear and warm. **Tennis** is available at several hotels and clubs on the island; **golf** is offered at Caye Chapel Island Resort, and there is a 9-hole course on the mainland near Belmopan, and two small 9-hole courses in the Corozal Town area.

Taxes: A 9% hotel tax is added to your hotel charges. The 10% Goods and Services Tax (GST) included on most goods and services, including tours and dive trips. Visitors departing Belize by international air pay taxes and fees totaling US$39.25 (some airlines include this tax in the ticket price.) Those departing Belize by land or boat (not by cruise ship) pay US$18.75 in border fees.

Taxis: As you walk around San Pedro, drivers will ask if you need a taxi. Your hotel also can call a taxi for you. Rates on the island are about US$3 to $10, depending on distance. The $10 rate (for the taxi, not per person) is for trips to the southern-most hotels such as Pelican Reef. Auto taxis do not go to North Ambergris. A scheduled water taxi service, **Island Ferry** (tel. 501-226-3231) operates roughly hourly from 7 a.m. to 10 p.m. **Coastal Xpress** (tel. 501-226-2006) is a new ferry service competing with Island Ferry. Rates vary but generally range from US$7 to $25, depending on the destination. You pay in advance. Some hotels and condos on North Ambergris offer free water shuttles for guests.

Telephones: Belize has **good telephone service,** both internally and internationally, with fiber optic cables and other modern technology. However, calling costs, especially internationally, are high. A seven-digit dialing system was introduced in 2002. You can visit the BTL Web site at www.btl.net, and look up numbers in the directory database. **When dialing from outside Belize, you must also dial the country code and international calling prefix. The country code for Belize is 501. When dialing from the U.S., add 011**, so to call a regular number in San Pedro from the U.S. dial 011-501-xxx-xxxx. To call the U.S. from San Pedro, dial 001 + Area Code + 7-digit number.

Pay phones in San Pedro and all over Belize operate only with a prepaid BTL calling card. These cards are sold in many shops in denominations from BZ$10 to $50.
It costs about US$50 for BTL to install a telephone in your home, plus a US$100 refundable deposit. If you are not a citizen or official resident, the deposit jumps to US$500. There is a US$10 a month residential service fee.

Local calls in Belize are charged by the minute (each local minute costs US 5 cents, after some free units.) Costs for calls to other parts of Belize vary from US 10 to 20 cents a minute during the day, and half that at night. A 10-minute daytime call from San Pedro to Belize City is US$1. Costs of direct-dialed long-distance calls to the U.S. currently are US 80 cents a minute, less at night. Local cybercafes charge around BZ$1 a minute for phone calls to the U.S. or Canada, and may give a free 5-minute call if you buy a drink. *(See also Cell Phones above.)*

With costs so high, many in Belize turned to VoIP technology, such as that offered by Vonage and Skype, to cut long-distance costs. VoIP uses the internet to make long-distance calls, at a fraction of the regular cost, and in the case of peer-to-peer computer services such as Skype, for no cost. However, for those with a BTL telephone number or DSL service, BTL has been blocking access to many of these sites. A ruling in mid-2006 by the Public Utilities Commission specifically permitted the use of Category 1 (computer-to-computer) VoIP services such as Skype in Belize, but BTL wants to block services that involve a telephone number separate from the computer to computer service. SmartNet does not block VoIP.

Tennis: The tennis options on the island are growing. At present, there are courts at **Journey's End Resort, Seascape** and **Belizean Shores** on North Ambergris, at the **Belize Yacht Club** south of town and at the **San Pedro Fitness Club**. There also are courts at San Pedro High School.

Time: Belize is on Central Standard Time and does not observe daylight savings time.

Tipping: With tourism being the number one industry on the island, tipping is common. Some hotels add a 5% to 10% service charge to your bill; if yours does not, you should leave something for the housekeepers, around US$2 per day being typical. In better restaurants, a 10% to 15% tip is usual, with more for exceptional service. Taxi drivers (car or boat) are not tipped. Tour and snorkel guides usually expect a tip, which varies depending on length and type of trip, but use 10% of the trip cost as a guideline.

Visitor Information: One of the best sources of current information about this island is on the Internet. Marty Casado's site,

AmbergrisCaye.com (www.ambergriscaye.com), has thousands of pages of information about San Pedro. The **Belize Tourism Board** also has some information on San Pedro. The BTB's office is at 64 Regent Street in Belize City (write P.O. Box 325, Belize City); e-mail info@travelbelize.org, tel. 501-227-2420. The BTB's Web site is at www.travelbelize.org.

Water to Drink: **On most of the island, you can drink the water and have ice in your drinks without worrying.** The town of San Pedro has a municipal water supply with chlorinated water that is safe to drink. Outside of town, hotels and houses get water from shallow wells – the water is usually okay but may taste brackish. Cisterns also provide some water. You can buy bottled water from all local groceries and shops. Ice at hotels and restaurants is almost always made from purified water. Most visitors eat and drink as they would at home and do not have stomach problems.

Water Taxis to Belize City and Caye Caulker: Two water taxi companies, with fast boats that hold up to 100 passengers, connect Belize City with Ambergris Caye (US$12.50 one-way) and Caye Caulker (US$7.50 one-way), each with eight to ten departures a day. **Caye Caulker Water Taxi** boats depart from the Marine Terminal near the Swing Bridge; **San Pedro Belize Express** aka **San Pedro Water Jets Express** boats leave from the nearby Brown Sugar building near the Tourism Village dock. It's a 45-minute ride to Caulker and 75 minutes to San Pedro. Boats stop on demand at Caye Chapel. *(Also see the Getting to San Pedro section below; for information on water taxis on Ambergris, see Taxis above.)*

GETTING TO SAN PEDRO

Getting to San Pedro is easy as caye lime pie, but it does require at least one stop along the way. There is no international air service direct to San Pedro's little 3,000 foot airstrip. **Continental, Delta, US Air, American** and **TACA** fly nonstop into the International Airport at Ladyville just north of Belize City from several U.S. gateways: Continental from Houston and Newark, Delta from Atlanta, US Air from Charlotte, TACA from Houston and American from Dallas-Fort Worth and Miami. Seasonally there are charter flights to Belize from Toronto via Roatan, Honduras. At times, there also are weekly flights from Havana, Cuba. With the runway extension project at the international airport completed, Belize is hoping to get service from Europe, but as of this writing nothing has been announced. Belize's International Airport also has service from San Pedro Sula, Honduras; Flores, Guatemala; Cancun, Mexico; Guatemala City; and San Salvador, El Salvador.

From Belize City: **You can either fly or take a water taxi to San Pedro (or to Caye Caulker).** It's a 20-minute flight to San Pedro; the boat trip takes about 75 minutes. To Caulker, it's 10 minutes by air, 45 minutes by boat. Two Belize airlines, **Maya Island Air** and **Tropic Air,** each have about one flight per hour every day to San Pedro, starting at around 7:30 a.m. and ending around 5:30 p.m. In peak visitor season, sometimes additional flights are added to accommodate demand. Flights originate from both the International Airport in Ladyville about 9 miles north of Belize City, where your international flight arrives, and Municipal Airport, a small airstrip in Belize City. In many cases the same Maya Island and Tropic flight picks up passengers at both airports, making the short hop between the two in a few minutes. Most flights also stop at Caye Caulker on demand.

Should you fly to San Pedro from International or Municipal? Depends on whether you'd rather save time or money. It's easier just to fly into International and walk over to the domestic terminal and catch your connecting puddle jumper. But you'll save a little money, especially if traveling in a party of several people, by flying from Municipal. Adult and child one-way fares on both Maya Island and Tropic are approximately US$63 from International; from Municipal, adult one-way is US$35. Round-trip fares are just slightly less than twice one-way. Only rarely are there any bargain fares or discounts for advance booking. Sometimes, mainly in the summer, the Belize airlines will offer deals if you pay cash, rather than use a credit card. Fares to Caulker are the same as to San Pedro.

Transferring between the airports requires a 20-minute taxi ride. A taxi from International to Municipal is US$25 for up to four or five passengers. A tip isn't necessary unless the driver carries a lot of your luggage, in which case add a couple of bucks. Taxis – they have green license tags – are plentiful and await passengers just outside the main lobby.

A party of four pays about US$480 round-trip to San Pedro via International, and US$318 round-trip from Municipal, even including the taxi transfers.

Do you need to make reservations for Maya Island or Tropic flights in advance? Off-season, it's not really necessary, though having a reservation won't hurt. In-season, a reservation might save a wait. Most hotels on Ambergris Caye will arrange for your air travel to the island at the time you make your hotel reservations, and there's usually no extra cost to you. The hotel gets a small commission from the airline.

You also can book direct with the airlines by telephone or over the Internet. Here's contact information:

Maya Island Air: 800-225-6732 or 501-226-3838, fax 226-2192; schedules, fares and reservations at www.mayaregional.com.

Tropic Air: 800-422-3435 or 501-226-2012; schedules, fares and reservations at www.tropicair.com.

Astrum Helicopters (tel. 501-222-9462, www.astrumhelicopters.com) near Belize City offers VIP transfers of guests to selected hotels, including Turneffe Island Resort, Turneffe Flats, Cayo Espanto, Azul Resort, Isla Marisol, Chaa Creek and Maruba Jungle Lodge & Spa, all of which have heliports. Astrum also offers helicopter charters, tours, and aerial photography trips, plus medivac service.

Another option is to take a water taxi or ferry from Belize City to San Pedro. If you are going to San Pedro or Caye Caulker, you have the option of taking a water taxi. Two water taxi companies, with fast boats that hold up to 100 passengers, connect Belize City with Ambergris Caye (US$12.50 one-way) and Caye Caulker (US$7.50 one-way), each with eight to ten departures a day. Caye Caulker Water Taxi boats depart from the Marine Terminal near the Swing Bridge; San Pedro Belize Express boats leave from Brown Sugar building near the Tourism Village. Despite their names, both water taxi companies have service to both Caye Caulker and San Pedro. It's a 45-minute ride to Caulker and 75 minutes to San Pedro. Boats stop on demand at Caye Chapel. You can make reservations, but boarding is likely to be first-come, first-served. A cab to downtown Belize City from the International Airport is about 20 minutes and US$25.

Coming from Mexico or Northern Belize: The cheapest way to get to Belize is often not to fly to Belize but to fly to **Cancun** (or sometimes Cozumel/Playa del Carmen) and then bus (if from Coz, ferry first) from there. There are many charter flights into Cancun from the U.S., Canada and even Europe, often at fares that are one-third to one-half what they are into Belize. From Cancun or Playa, you can take a bus to Chetumal (four and a half to six hours and US$20 or less for a nice, comfortable reserved seat, with A/C and videos).

An option that became available in 2009 is to fly from Cancun to Belize City on **Maya Island Air** (www.mayaregional.com). Currently there is one daily flight.

Another new option is to take a water taxi, operated by **San Pedro Water Jets Express**, formerly San Pedro-Belize Express, (www.sanpedrowatertaxi.com) direct from Chetumal to San Pedro. It leaves from the **Muelle Fiscal** (municipal pier) and costs US$35 one-way. Currently there is one boat a day in the mid-afternoon, but schedules change frequently.

Most travelers, however, will come through the border at Chetumal and Corozal Town. To get to San Pedro or Caye Caulker, you have several options:

1) Take **ADO** or another Mexican bus line from Playa del Carmen or Cancun to Chetumal (generally US$20 or less, depending on the class of service and the peso exchange rate). Many people prefer to hop a bus from the Cancun International Airport to Playa (about US$9 or less) and from there take ADO or CCO to Chetumal. Most buses from Playa to Chetumal leave from the newer Playa bus station, not the older one near the waterfront. For information on Mexican bus schedules, visit **Ticketbus** (www.ticketbus.com.mx). To Chetumal, it is about six hours from Cancun and less than four and a half hours from Playa.

In Chetumal, you'll transfer to a Belize bus. With the breakup of Novelo's bus line, bus service in Belize is now fragmented among a number of small bus lines, and schedules and even the names of the bus lines can change. However, when you arrive in Chetumal just ask about a bus to Belize, and you'll have no problem finding one. Some buses -- typically they are old U.S. school buses -- leave from the main ADO terminal, but some leave from the Nuevo Mercado area, a short taxi ride from the ADO station. Cross the border - the bus waits as you go through both Mexican and Belizean customs and immigration. Cost to Corozal Town is US$1.50. Note: From Chetumal, you can also hire a taxi or transfer to take you across the border, instead of taking a bus, with the rate negotiable, but usually around US$30 per person, not including any border fees. Then, from Corozal Town, continue down the Northern Highway (around US$6 and 3 to 3 1/2 hours) to Belize City, and from there take a water taxi *(see above)* or flight to San Pedro.

Another bus option is to take a tourist bus, such as **Linea Dorada,** which runs from Chetumal to Flores, Guatemala, stopping at the Marine Terminal in Belize City. The fare from Chet to Flores is around US$35, and from the Marine Terminal to Flores US$20 to $25.

2) Transfer services in Corozal and elsewhere in Belize will also pick you up in Cancun or elsewhere in Mexico and bring you to Corozal or to Belize City.   **Belize VIP Transfer Service,** formerly Menzies Tours (www.belizetransfers.com, tel. 501-422-2725) is one of these. You'll pay US400 for up to four persons from Cancun to Corozal, US$350 from Playa del Carmen, US$300 from Tulum, and US$45 from Bacalar. Other shuttle services also operate.

3) You now have the option to take a water taxi from Corozal directly to San Pedro. Most of the year, there's only one boat a day, operated by San Pedro Belize Express. It departs Corozal from the pier near Reunion Park at 7 a.m. and returns from San Pedro at 3 p.m. It stops at Sarteneja on demand. Fare is US$22.50 one-way, US$40 round-trip. (Check departure times

locally, as they may change, and service may be limited or non-existent off-season. A second boat may be added during high season.) The trip takes around two hours, longer if it's bad weather or if there's a long stop at Sarteneja. It can be a butt-buster.

4) Have the bus from Chetumal drop you at the Coro airstrip, or take a taxi to the airstrip and fly to San Pedro, a trip that takes about 25 minutes. **Tropic Air** has six flights a day to San Pedro, currently at 7:30, 9:30, 11:30, 1:30, 3:30, and 5:15 for US$47.50 one-way. **Maya Island Air** has several flights a day, for about the same pricew. .

OVERNIGHTING IN COROZAL TOWN

There's not a lot to do in Corozal, but it's a fun place not to do it. If you stay over in Corozal, here are recommended hotels. Note: Corozal Town was sideswiped by Hurricane Dean in August 2007, but mainly just lost a few trees.

★★★★ **Serenity Sands B&B.** Mile 3, Consejo Rd. (P.O. Box 88, Corozal Town), 501-669-2394; www.serenitysands.com. This new B&B is hidden away off the Consejo Road north of Corozal Town. On the second floor of a large home, there are four tastefully decorated rooms with private balconies, Belizean art and locally made hardwood furniture. Although not directly on the water, Serenity has a private beach on the bay a few hundred feet away. Rates are an excellent value for the high quality you enjoy, from US$75 plus tax. Full breakfasts, mostly organic, are included. For families, there's a 2-bedroom cottage near the B&B. Best visited with a rental car.

★★★★ **Almond Tree Resort.** 425 Bayshore Dr., South End, 501-628-9224; www.almondtreeresort.com. New small inn is a fine upscale choice at reasonable rates. Almond Tree has a sparkling fresh water pool and a sandy beach. There are six rooms all with queen beds, 1 large suite with separate living room and panoramic views of Corozal Bay, 2 smaller suites. Room rates vary between US$75 and $125 in season, double occupancy. This includes morning coffee, tea, juice, yogurt and fruit. There is air conditioning in rooms, hot water, cable TV, laundry services, bikes and wireless access throughout premises. Restaurant and bar coming.

★★★+ **Casablanca by the Sea.** Consejo Village; tel. 501/423-1018; www.casablanca-bythesea.com. This little inn out Consejo way doesn't get as many guests as it deserves, but it's a fine little getaway. It's a great place to just relax and do nothing. The views of Chetumal across Corozal Bay are terrific. Rooms are around US$75 double.

★★★+ **Corozal Bay Resort.** Almond Dr., South end of Corozal Town, next to Tony's Inn; tel. 501/422-2691; www.corozalbayinn.com. Doug and Maria — she's originally from Mexico, and he's a Canadian by birth of German heritage who moved to Belize with his family when he was a youngster — have built 10 attractive cabañas on the water. The cabañas, painted in colorful tropical pastels, are surprisingly spacious and have bay thatch roofs. While most of them are situated to catch the breeze from the bay, they do have air-conditioning, tile baths, two comfortable beds in each cabaña, and 27" TVs with cable. Two units at the back connect, making them ideal for families. Doug had several hundred dump truck loads of sand brought in and created a tropical beach on the bay. There is a seawall, but you'll love the water view and the concrete pier. You can sit by the pool, sip something cold in the redone outdoor restaurant and bar and, if you have a wireless laptop, check your e-mail. Rates are US$60 to $70 double. New budget rooms are under construction.

★★★ **Copa Banana Guesthouse.** 409 Bay Shore Drive., P.O. Box 226, Corozal Town, tel. 501-422-0284, fax 422-2710; www.copabanana.bz. Whether you're just passing through or in town shopping for property around Corozal, you couldn't do much better than this guesthouse. The rates are affordable, you can cook meals in the common kitchen, complete with dishware, stove, coffeemaker, microwave and fridge, and the owners even run a real estate business, Belize North Real Estate Ltd. Connie and her partner, Gregg, have done up two banana-yellow one-story, ranch-style concrete houses, with a total of five rooms (some with queen beds, some with two twins). Guests have private bedrooms but share the common space. The owners have added a long-term rental apartment with a view of the bay. Rates: US$55 double/US$350 week.

★★★ **Tony's Inn.** South End, Corozal Town; tel. 501-422-2055 or 800-447-2931; fax 422-2829; www.tonysinn.com. A long-time favorite of travelers to Corozal, Tony's has 24 motel-like rooms with tile floors, cable TV and A/C. The breezy bayside palapa restaurant, Y Not Grill, is one of the best in town -- try the fajitas. Rates: US$80 double January-April, US$70 rest of the year.

★★+ **Las Palmas.** 123 5th Ave., Corozal Town; tel. 501-422-0196; www.laspalmashotelbelize.com. This was formerly the budget-level Nestor's Hotel. It has been totally renovated and rebuilt, moving the whole property upmarket. Rooms go for about US$40 to $50 a night, double. Las Palmas is currently for sale.

★★ **Sea Breeze Hotel.** 23 1st Ave., tel. 501-422-3051; www.theseabreezehotel.com. The Sea Breeze, currrently for sale, is your best budget choice in Corozal, with rooms starting at US$20 plus tax. The green-and-white painted building, for-merly a Catholic nunnery, is across the street from the bay, behind a concrete wall. Inside, you'll find comfortable, no-frills guest rooms and a well-stocked bar (for guests and friends of guests only). Breakfast, at one of the lowest prices in Corozal, is served, also for guests only. Rooms are simple and can be hot.

OVERNIGHTING IN BELIZE CITY

Most visitors to San Pedro are able to get to the island without an overnight in Belize City. If you stay over in Belize City, here are recommended hotels:

Downtown Area

★★★★+ **Great House,** 13 Cork St.; tel. 501-223-3400, fax 223-3444; www.greathousebelize.com.   This small jewel offers spacious and well-equipped air-conditioned rooms in a modernized and expanded private house, originally built in 1927. All 12 rooms, half on the second and half on the third floor, have a balcony, private bathroom, mini-fridge, safe, TV, phone and dedicated fax line. There is also a good, if somewhat pricey, restaurant in the courtyard, the **Smoky Mermaid.** Owner Steve Maestre takes great pride in the personal service here. Doubles around US$110-$130.

★★★★ **Radisson Fort George,** 2 Marine Parade; tel. 501-223-3333, fax 227-3829; www.radissonbelize.com.   This is the flagship of the city's hotels, and the most expensive, though you can often get substantial reductions from the rack rates. All rooms have cable TV, fridge and minibar, and those in the Club Wing, reached by the only glass elevator in Belize, have unbeatable sea views. Most of the rooms, including those in the villa wing across the street, have been remodeled recently. There are good restaurants, and the grounds are an oasis of calm on the edge of the sea. The hotel has two pools and a private dock. The marina can take large boats of up to 250 feet in length with a 10-foot draft. The staff is usually friendly and helpful. Rates US$169-189 double, Dec. 20-Apr. 30, about US$10 less the rest of year. But as noted, rates are often heavily discounted – ask.

★★+ **Hotel Mopan.** 55 Regent St., Belize City; tel. 501-227-7351, fax 227-5383; www.hotelmopan.com.   Character is the Hotel Mopan's middle name. This hotel in an old wooden Colonial house on the South Side became a well-known meeting place for naturalists, archeologists and backpackers under pioneering tourism operator Jean Shaw, who died in 1999. Her daughter and son, Jeannie and Tomy, operate the hotel today. Don't expect luxury here, and the neighborhood isn't exactly grand (walking around at night is iffy at best), but the rooms are bigger than average, they've been upgraded and there's still lots of atmosphere. All rooms have private baths with plenty of hot water, and A/C is available. Rates US$50 to $70 double.

Near International Airport/Midway to City Centre
★★★★ **D'Nest Inn.** 475 Cedar St. tel. 501/223-5416; www.dnestinn.com. (Directions: from the Northern Hwy., turn west on Chetumal St., turn right at the police station, go 1 block and turn left, then turn right on Cedar St.) D'Nest Inn is a B&B run by Gaby and Oty Ake. Gaby is a retired Belize banker, and Oty is originally from Chetumal. The two-story, Caribbean-style house is on a canal 50 feet from the Belize River. It's in an area called Belama Phase 2, a safe, middle-class section between the international airport and downtown. Oty's gardens around the house are filled with hibiscus, roses and other blossoming plants. The four guest rooms are furnished with antiques such as a hand-carved, four-poster bed, but they also have modcons like wireless internet, air-conditioning and cable TV. With a private entrance and your own key, you come and go as you like. Rates are US$60 to $70 plus tax double and include a delicious full breakfast. *Highly recommended.*

★★ **Global Village Hotel.** Mile 8 1/2, Northern Hwy.; tel. 501/225-2555; www.globalhotel-bz.com. If you have an early morning flight out or you're overnighting en route somewhere else, the Global Village Hotel (actually, it's more of a motel than a hotel) is a good choice near the international airport. The 40 rooms are sparkling clean and modern and are only US$50 double. This Chinese-owned place is located just south of the turnoff to the international airport, and the hotel has a free shuttle to and from the airport. You can also arrange to leave your car in the hotel's fenced parking lot with 24-hour security.

WOW! FIRST IMPRESSIONS OF SAN PEDRO

Your first impression of Ambergris Caye is likely to be from the air, because most visitors to the island fly to San Pedro.

As you fly the 35 miles to San Pedro, your little plane soars over several islands, including **Hen and Chicken Cayes**, the larger **Hick's Cayes**, and then **Caye Chapel** (site of Belize's only 18-hole golf course). The large caye just north of Chapel is Caye Caulker, the second-most developed and most-populated of Belize's islands after Ambergris. Some flights make a brief stop at Caulker before going on to San Pedro. Leonardo DiCaprio has purchased **Blackadore Caye** on the back side of Ambergris Caye and may open a resort there. A development plan has been filed.

On a clear day, you get a great introduction to Belize's Caribbean Coast. As your plane goes low over the transparent water, you'll see mangrove – or sand – edged islands, coral heads, the sand and sea grass bottom, fishing boats and sometimes the blur of large fish.

You'll come in over the south end of the island. **Hol Chan**

Marine Reserve, a popular snorkeling site, is just off the southeast tip of Ambergris. A few houses dot the southern coast of the island, becoming more densely clustered as you approach the town. The group of small houses in a muddy flat just south of the airport were built to house local residents after Hurricane Keith. Just a few hundred yards off the east side of the island is the barrier reef. From the air, the sea is usually clear as glass; the water inside the reef has a green or turquoise tint, while on the ocean side it is a deeper blue and, on stormy or overcast days, it can take on a purple hue, like an angry bruise.

Ambergris Caye isn't a large island. It's 25 miles long and only 4 miles wide at its widest point, about one-half the size of Barbados. Much of the island is low mangrove swamp, and there are a dozen lagoons.

The air strip, around 3,000 feet long, comes into view and within seconds you're on the ground. As you taxi to the small airline buildings at the north end of the air strip, including the new Tropic Air terminal, you'll see, in the bright glare of the sun, the southern end of San Pedro Town. Several popular hotels and condotels are at this end of town. Most resorts meet arriving guests in a car or golf cart, but if yours doesn't, you can take a taxi or, if staying nearby, make the short walk.

A TOUR OF THE ISLAND

The experienced Caribbean traveler will recognize San Pedro Town immediately: In some ways, it's the Caribbean of 30 years ago, before the boom in international travel, a throwback to the days before cruise ships turned too many Caribbean islands into concrete mini-malls hustling duty-free booze and discount jewelry. There are just three north-south streets. Wood houses and shops, painted in bright tropical colors fading quickly in the sun, stand close together. Newer buildings are reinforced concrete, optimistically girded for the next big hurricane.

Foot and bicycle traffic predominate, though the streets are busy with golf carts – keep a close eye, as the electric ones sneak up behind you silently – and, unfortunately, an ever increasing number of pickups and cars.

The name of **Front Street** (dozens of Caribbean islands have main streets named Front, Middle and Back) was changed a few years ago to the more romantic-sounding **Barrier Reef Drive**. It is one-way, with carts and vehicles allowed to go north only for most of its distance, to **Caribena Street**. On weekends, the street is closed to all but pedestrians. **Middle Street**, or **Pescador Drive**, is one-way south from the intersection with Caribena Street.

Many hotels, restaurants and larger businesses are on Front Street. Just beyond the primary school and the bite-sized San Pedro Library (here, you don't need a library card, and even visitors can check out books, free, or a buy a used paperback for a dollar or two), you'll see **Rubie's**, also spelled Ruby's, **Sea Gal, Celi's Deli, Holiday Hotel**, **Spindrift,** home of the chicken

Beachfront in San Pedro

drop, and then, near "Central Park." **Big Daddy's** and **Jaguar's** clubs are across the street from each other, and the Catholic church, cool and welcoming, stands guard. Farther up on the right there's **Fido's**, a popular bar and restaurant, and the **Mayan Princess**. On the left is the big, modern **Belize Bank** building. As Barrier Reef Drive peters out, dead ahead is **SeaBreeze Suites,** the new **Phoenix** condos and comfy **Paradise Villas.**

To the east, beyond the line of buildings, only a few feet away, accessible through many alleys, is the Caribbean. There's a narrow strip of beach and seawall between the buildings and the sea, used as a pedestrian walkway. A number of piers or docks jut out into the sea. The patch of white you see a few hundred yards out is surf breaking over the barrier reef.

Even if you're a strong swimmer, don't try swimming out to the reef from the shore, especially not in or near town. There is a lot of boat traffic inside the reef, and over the years several swimmers have been killed or injured by boats.

Middle Street, or Pescador Drive, the other main north-south venue, is also busy. It's home to several restaurants, including **Elvi's Kitchen, Cocina Caramba, The Reef** and other worthies. As you go farther north on Middle Street, San Pedro becomes more residential, and more local. You'll see the **San Pedro Supermarket** (which usually has better prices than the larger Island Supermarket south of town), electric and telephone facilities, a small high school, playground, and then the Boca del Rio or "the river" or "the channel."

Cross the New Bridge to North Ambergris

In early 2006, a **new bridge** opened over the river. Until then, you crossed the channel on a hand-pulled ferry. The bridge is for golf carts, bikes and pedestrians only. Golf carts are charged BZ$5 each way, pedestrians BZ$1. For longer-term stays you can buy a monthly pass.) A small golf cart and walking path wends its way north, mostly on the back side of the island, past several planned and under-construction condo developments, expat homes, restaurants and resorts. The cart path, badly washed when it rains, is often bumpy and muddy. Plans are afoot to improve it. You can usually drive your cart past **Captain Morgan's**, made briefly famous by the *Temptation Island* reality TV program and still abuilding with new timeshares and condos, as far as **Belizean Shores, Seascape**, **Las Terrazas, Journey's End Resort**, **Rendezvous** restaurant, **Rojo Lounge** and **Azul Resort**,

Bay thatch awaiting transport to someone's roof

Portofino and **Mata Chica**. You can actually go all the way to Robles Point beyond **Blue Reef Island Resort.** But it is a long, long drive, some of it inland and some on the beach, which unfortunately is littered with trash in many places. After rains, the cart path this far north may be impassable.

Be sure to take plenty of bug spray, and wear light-colored clothes, because on North Ambergris away from the water, mosquitoes can be terrible, especially in the late summer and fall, after seasonal rains.

Beyond most of the resorts is a large area that is beginning to develop for private homes, but some of it is undeveloped. Over the years, many schemes have been floated for this part of the island, once part of a private holding called the Pinkerton Estate. A large chunk of this area has been saved from Cancunization thanks to establishment of the **Bacalar Chico** national park and marine reserve. The park, which opened in 1996, comprises 12,000 acres of land and 15,000 acres of water. At present the park is accessible by boat from San Pedro, from the Belize mainland at **Sarteneja** and elsewhere and from the Mexican port village of **Xcalak**. The park is home to a surprisingly large population of birds and wildlife, and there are a number of Maya sites. This northern tip of the island is separated from the Mexican Yucatán only by the narrow Bacalar Chico channel. Indeed, Ambergris Caye once was physically part of the Yucatán peninsula, the channel having been dug by the Maya. In recent years, several remote beachfront resorts have opened some 8 to 12 miles north of town, including **Blue Reef, Salamander Hideaway** and **Tranquility**.

Heading South

Head south from town rather than north, and you're on **Coconut Drive.** A cluster of hotels and other businesses are near the airstrip, including **SunBreeze, The Palms** and **Ramon's Village,** with its annex, the cleverly named **Steve & Becky's Cute Little Hotel**, painted in bright Caribbean colors, on the right side of the street. Coconut Drive is now paved with concrete cobblestones all the way to Victoria House. You'll pass the **Belize Yacht Club, Changes in Latitudes B&B, Exotic Caye** with its thatch condos, **Corona Del Mar, Coconuts Hotel** and **Caribbean Villas.** You'll also see the **Island Supermarket,** San Pedro's largest, spiffiest grocery, and soft-drink and beer magnate Barry Bowen's turf, which includes **Island Academy,** one of the better private schools in Central America, and his warehouse facility. At the warehouse you can buy Belikin, soft drinks and bottled water by the case for less than you'd pay in groceries. Some of the buildings, you'll note, are painted Belikin green.

The road veers sharply right, then back left. The area west of the main drag here, or to your right going south, is the San Pablo residential area, and on the lagoon a cluster of cheap pre-fab homes put up by the government in a flood plain, after Hurricane Keith. San Pablo is starting to become a tourist area, too.

Considerable development is taking place along the sea, and there's no telling what a seafront foot would cost you here now. **Villas at Banyan Bay,** now taken over by its lender, Belize Bank, with the newer **Grand Colony** condos (they start at over half a million US), **Banana Beach** (under new Canadian owner-ship)**, Mata Rock, Royal Palm,** the beautifully upgraded **Victoria House, Royal Caribbean, Sunset Beach**, **Miramar** and **Pelican Reef** are also in this area.   By this point, you're some 3 miles south of San Pedro Town. If you continue farther south, by foot or cart, you're back in a residential area, with a number of upmarket houses including one owned by musician Jerry Jeff Walker, along with shacks, mansions and other assort-ed digs.

WHAT IT COSTS TO VACATION HERE

Is a vacation on Ambergris Caye expensive?

Yes and no. Compared to a stay in an out-of-the-way hotel in Panama or on the Caribbean Coast of Nicaragua, San Pedro is expensive. Compared with St. Barts or Anguilla in the Caribbean, it is cheap.

Overall, excluding airfare, a vacation in San Pedro costs about the same as a vacation in Florida. On Ambergris, as in Florida, there's a range of vacation costs, depending on whether you're staying at budget hotels and eating burritos, or staying in beachfront resorts and dining well.

Here's an estimate of what it costs, for a week's vacation, per couple, at budget, moderate and luxury levels. This is based on two people traveling together, in-season (December to Easter). You can get by on somewhat less, or spend a good deal more. Off-season, the hotel may cost 20% to 40% less, but other items will be about the same. Figures shown are estimates and don't include air fare to Belize. Hotel rates include service, if any, and hotel tax. A single person would pay about 10% less for the hotel room, but other charges would generally be cut in half. Budgets do not include air fare from the U.S. or Canada, which would typically run US$800 to $1,400 per couple, depending on the city of origin.

Budget Level

(Per Couple for Week's Vacation)

Buses between International Airport and Belize City	US$ 8
Water taxis between Belize City and San Pedro	US$60
Room at a budget hotel	US$225
Meals at budget restaurants and street vendors	US$240
Entertainment (informal activities; rum drinks	

A temple at Tikal, reachable on a day trip by air from San Pedro

at local bars)	US$100
1 snorkel trip for two	US$50
1 day trip to Altun Ha	US$135
1 day bicycle rental	US$20
Miscellaneous (tips, personal purchases, fees)	US$80
Belize departure taxes and fees	US$80
Total:	**US$997 for two**

Moderate Level

(Per Couple for Week's Vacation)

Taxis between International and Municipal	US$50
Round-trip air fare between Municipal Airport and San Pedro	US$134
Room at attractive mid-priced beachfront hotel	US$850
Meals at moderate restaurants	US$350

Entertainment (drinks, dancing)	US$200
1 snorkel trip for two	US$50
2 two-tank dives for two	US$280
1 day's golf cart rental	US$65
1 day cruise	US$110
1 day excursion to Altun Ha	US$135
Miscellaneous	US$150
Belize departure taxes and fees	US$80

Total: **US$2,454 for two**

Luxury Level

(Per Couple for Week's Vacation)

Round-trip air fare between Belize International and San Pedro (for two)	US$240
Room at upmarket resort	US$1900
Meals at moderate and expensive restaurants	US$900
Entertainment (drinks, dancing)	US$400
2 snorkel trips for two	US$100
Atoll/Blue Hole diving trip for two	US$500
2 days' golf cart rental	US$120
1 day excursion to Lamanai	US$250
1 day fishing charter	US$300
1 day trip via air to Tikal plus miscellaneous charges	US$550
Miscellaneous	US$300
Belize departure taxes and fees	US$80

Total: **US$5,640 for two**

SUGGESTED ITINERARY FOR A WEEK

Day One: Relax. Decompress. Forget about the real world. Take a lazy walk through town.

Day Two: Relax some more. Take a snorkel trip to Hol Chan and Shark-Sting Ray Alley (or go diving).

Day Three: Bike or cart to North Ambergris (if not staying there). Walk the beach and have lunch at one of the North End beach hotels or have a seaside picnic.

Day Four: Take a day trip to Lamanai or Altun Ha ruins or go cave tubing.

Day Five: Take a catamaran or other boat trip to Caye Caulker and other islands, or take a day trip to the Belize Zoo and Western Belize.

Day Six: Relax by the pool. Take a snorkel trip to Mexico Rocks (or go diving.)

Day Seven: Relax and start worrying again about going back the real world.

EVERYTHING YOU NEED TO KNOW ABOUT AMBERGRIS CAYE

Here's what you need to know about the island to enjoy it fully.

ISLAND HISTORY

Maya Indians were the first residents of Ambergris Caye. Some of their history is told in small ruins still remaining, including the Marco Gonzales site near the south tip of the island and several sites in Bacalar Chico park in the north. There are few Mayas on the caye today, however.

The village of San Pedro was founded in 1848 by refugees from the Caste Wars in the Yucatán. The Caste Wars were a series of successful rebellions by the Maya against the Spanish, and the

Indian armies drove thousands of Mexicans south to Belize. The Mestizos who settled San Pedro were mostly fishermen (hence the name of the village, after St. Peter the Fisherman) and farmers, and they continued this work on Ambergris Caye. Many native San Pedranos today can trace their ancestry back to the Caste Wars immigration. At home and among themselves, these families, with surnames such as Guerrero, Gomez and Nuñez, speak Spanish, though they are equally fluent in English. They control the island's politics, along with many of its small businesses.

SAN PEDRANOS AND EXPATS

Ambergris Caye has more foreign residents than any other area of Belize, but no one knows the exact number. It's somewhere around 2,000, although not all are full-time residents. The number is growing almost daily. The problem is: How and whom do you count? Are the snowbird couple from Michigan who own a condo on the island and spend winters in it residents or just visitors? Is the guy who has been here six months and tends bar on the side a local or a beach bum? How about the yachties with their catamaran tied up at a dock? Quite a large number of expats on the island are perpetual tourists, in Belize on a visitors card and here until their money, or perhaps their livers, run out.

Many of the island's resorts are owned and operated by expats from the U.S., Canada or the U.K. Other expats operate bars, restaurants, dive shops, gift shops, sailing charters, the island's ferry boat service and other small businesses. Selling real estate is a popular option for new arrivals.

While there is occasional friction between the local and expat communities, usually connected with development issues, most foreign residents have high regard for their local neighbors. San Pedranos are known for their friendly, easygoing ways, yet they don't fawn for the sake of a tip. Following years of good lobstering and growing tourism, many San Pedranos are financially comfortable, and a few who run successful businesses or who have sold beachfront land are well off by any standard. The island is Belize's biggest earner of hard currency, and it's a major exporter of tax revenues to Belmopan. Begging and beach hustling, other than by some timeshare hawkers, are virtually unknown on the island.

ISLAND FLORA

Ambergris Caye is a low-lying island, with no dramatic hills or mountains. **Coconut palms** - some of which are suffering from lethal yellowing disease - are the trees you will probably notice first. The island also has **saltwater palmettos** and other palms.

Mangroves - there are red, black and white mangroves here - are the most important trees on the island, because their root systems provide a home to a rich variety of sea life and literally prevent the island from being washed away. It is illegal to cut mangroves, but unfortunately this law is not always observed.

Sapodilla, the mimosa-like **acacia, coco plum** and large **Australian pines** are among other fairly common trees on Ambergris Caye. In gardens around town, you will see many tropical flowering plants such as **hibiscus, bougainvillea** and **poinsettia.**

This is not a lush jungle island, but there are many trees struggling to grow in the thin limestone soil and scrub vegetation in the sand.

CROCS, SHARKS AND OTHER CRITTERS

Despite development, Ambergris is still home to many wild creatures. The far north and south of the island have the most wild creatures. The sea, of course, is rich with life.

Small **whitetail deer** can occasionally be seen, along with **wild pigs** and **coatimundis** (locally called quash). Reportedly, three of Belize's five types of wild cats, the **marguay cat, jaguarundi** and the **ocelot** have been seen at the north of the island, but not, at least in recent times, the jaguar, though some island residents say jaguars have been spotted on North Ambergris. There are several kinds of sea turtles that come ashore on Ambergris Caye, mainly on the North End, the most common being the **loggerhead.** Around the island you may see the **common iguana** and also its smaller cousin, the **wish-willie,** or the Central American basilisk, frequently called the Jesus Christ lizard for its ability to run lightly across water.

Crocodiles lurk in the lagoons. Two species of crocodiles are found in Belize, and both can be seen on Ambergris Caye: the **American saltwater crocodile,** which can reach lengths of more than 21 feet, though one of that size has rarely if ever been found in Belize, and the smaller **Morelet's crocodile,** which rarely gets larger than 8 feet. Belizeans often refer to crocodiles as "alligators," but there are no true alligators in Belize. It is, by the way, illegal to eat crocodiles in Belize, so you won't find croc stew on restaurant menus. It's also illegal for you to feed them.

Are crocs dangerous to humans? You definitely wouldn't want to share a bathtub with one, but they rarely attack people. A Belizean youth was killed by an American crocodile in 2001, while swimming in a canal in Belize City. No human deaths from croc attacks have been reported on Ambergris Caye, although pet dogs have been killed.

More than 250 species of birds have been seen on Ambergris Caye. Non-birding visitors may especially note the **frigate birds** and **brown pelicans,** common around piers. Seagulls, oddly, are not very common. Elbert Greer, who writes a weekly column for the *San Pedro Sun* and who is author of a book on birding in Belize, *Birdwatching with Bubba,* and Susan Lala, former co-owner of Caribbean Villas, are among the island's resident birding experts.

It would takes pages to list all the undersea life around the island. Among the more interesting sea creatures are the

Dining at Elvi's in San Pedro

sharks. **Nurse sharks** are the most common, but **black-tip, lemon, tiger, bull** and even **hammerheads** come around. Bull sharks sometimes become a nuisance around the island, and they can be dangerous to humans. **Sting rays** are common, as are the larger **spotted eagle rays.** You will see many **barracuda,** prized by Belizeans as one of the best eating fish. Among sport and eating fish common around the island are **bone fish,** several types of **groupers, tarpon, marlin, wahoo** and **snappers. Spiny lobster** (legal season June 15 to February 15) and several varieties of **conch** (legal season October to June) are well known and delicious residents of the area. **Atlantic bottlenose dolphins** are often seen from the shore or following boats, and **manatees** may be seen on boat trips. The narrow beaches of Ambergris are not fertile territory for shelling, but shells can be found in the shallow water just off the beach. **Whale sharks,** the gentle giants of the sea, though more common farther south off Placencia, are occasionally seen off Ambergris Caye and Caye Caulker.

For detailed information on the natural history of Ambergris Caye, pick up a copy of *The Field Guide to Ambergris Caye* by R. L. Wood, S. T. Reid and A. M. Reid, may be available at shops on the island.

CREEPIE-CRAWLIES, BUGS AND BEES

Mosquito control efforts keep the mozzie problem to a minimum in San Pedro Town and the hotel areas to the south of town. Most visitors here aren't much bothered by either mosquitoes or **sandflies,** the pesky no-see-ums which sometimes plague visitors in other parts of Belize.

However, both on the north and the south ends of the island, especially away from the sea breezes and in summer after rainy periods, mosquitoes are plentiful. Even when you are riding in a golf cart, mosquitoes may swarm over you. The best protection is to spray with DEET. Bug juice with around 30% DEET is a good choice, although don't use concentrations of more than 10% on children. Repellants containing natural oil of lemon eucalyptus or the chemical picaridin also offer protection and may be less harsh to the skin than DEET. A university study has found that catnip oil is even more effective than DEET. And it could be true. After all, when was the last time you saw a mosquito bite a cat?

Africanized bees, tarantulas, scorpions and other creepie-crawlies do coexist with humans on Ambergris Caye, but it is rare that visitors will be bothered by them, or even see them. Supposedly two varieties of snakes are on the North End of island, a type of **boa constrictor** and the **black-tailed indigo**, neither one poisonous, but these are rarely seen.

MAYA SITES
The small **Marco Gonzales** Maya site is near the south tip of the island. It's not easy to find. Ask at your hotel for specific directions, and even then you probably will have no luck. A new pedestrian walkway and bridge to the site was planned but has never been constructed. Marco Gonzales is one of several mostly difficult-to-get-to sites on the island. Other small Maya sites on the island, which you can visit on boat tours to the North End, include **Chac Balam** and **Santa Cruz.**

To see larger, much more impressive Maya sites, you'll have to go to the mainland. Day trips to **Altun Ha, Lamanai, Tikal** and other sites are offered by several tour operators on the island. *(See Day Trips and Tours below.)*

BEAUTIFUL BEACHES
If you come to Ambergris Caye for wide, sandy beaches and terrific beach swimming, you may at first be a little disappoint-ed. Ambergris Caye hotel brochures tend to portray local beach-es with delighted couples frolicking on the sand, but the reality is that the island's beaches are mostly only narrow strips of sand along the eastern shore, sometimes held in place by a sea-wall. Water at the shore is shallow, and many areas have heavy eelgrass near shore or muddy bottoms, making swimming not always enjoyable. Seaweed and seagrass often pile up on

beaches, and the smell can be pungent. The seagrass, however, is part of the barrier reef ecology, acting as a nursery to sea life. On the beaches, it protects against erosion.

There is also an unfortunate amount of **garbage** on some of the beaches, some of it from local sources and much from boats or simply deposited by sea currents from other areas. Generally, hotel operators and home owners keep their beachfront areas clean, but undeveloped property often has trash on the beach. Some island residents also complain of trash dumped by the roadside, especially south of San Pedro town.

On the positive side, the view from the beaches of the turquoise water and barrier reef is spectacular, and at least when the off-shore prevailing winds are blowing, which is most of the time, there are few mosquitoes or no-see-ums to bother you. And even more Positively Front Street, there are no Aruba or Cancun-style highrises on the beach, or Jamaica-style higglers to bug you.

A number of hotels remove the **seagrass** from parts of their beach or from a swimming area at the end of their pier. While not a good move environmentally, this does make the swimming much more pleasant. In general, the farther north on the island you go, the less seagrass there is.

No one beach stands out as being vastly better than others. Indeed, except in areas of mangroves, there is a continuous narrow thread all along the Caribbean shore. For those in and near town, the **beach at Ramon's Village** is the best for swimming. Another good beach south of town is **Mar de Tumbo** near Grand Colony, Banyan Bay and Banana Beach. North Ambergris Caye has long stretches of tropically beautiful beach though, again, not especially wonderful for swimming.

CAUTION! Don't swim out too far from shore or in areas heavily used by power boats. Swimmers have been injured or killed in accidents with boats.

GREAT SNORKELING

Ambergris Caye offers superb snorkeling. Unfortunately, to enjoy it best you'll need to take a short boat trip out from shore.

You can snorkel off the beach at your hotel or anywhere on the island, but you don't usually see very much. Still, it can be pleasant to float around and see what you can see. A few areas on North Ambergris have some snorkeling close to shore. The **Basil Jones** area has coral heads close to shore, though the current here can be strong. At **Robles Point,** the reef is a couple of hundred feet from shore, and you can swim out. Getting to Robles Point and Basil Jones, however, requires a boat trip. Some beachfront hotels, including **Caribbean Villas** and **Ramon's,** have constructed **small artificial reefs** to attract fish for snorkelers.

The three most-popular areas for snorkeling from boats near Ambergris Caye are **Hol Chan Marine Reserve, Shark-Ray Alley** and **Mexico Rocks.** A visit to Hol Chan and Shark-Ray Alley to the south of San Pedro (Shark-Ray Alley is now officially a part of the Hol Chan reserve) are usually combined into one trip, while Mexico Rocks to the north of town is usually a separate trip.

The Hol Chan Marine Reserve, about 4 miles south of San Pedro, is a 5-square-mile underwater national park established by the Belize government in 1987. Because fishing is prohibited in the reserve, there is a considerable amount of sea life. At the cut here, you may expect to see large groupers, nurse sharks, sting rays, moray and other eels, spadefish, schoolmasters and other fish. Much of the bottom is sandy, but you also will see bright coral. Depth is fairly shallow at between 5 to 30 feet. Visibility is usually good, at 50 to 60 feet or more, with late spring having the best water viz.

You will not be alone. As many as 10 or 15 snorkel boats may congregate at one time. When cruise ships are in port in Belize City, the Hol Chan is particularly busy. In fact, it's a good idea to make a mental note of the name or identifying colors of your boat, so you don't swim back to the wrong boat. With so many snorkelers and divers - albeit the total number is nothing like that in popular snorkeling areas in Mexico or the United States Virgin Islands - the environment here has suffered some damage, despite the designation of the area as a reserve. Do not touch the coral with your hands or fins, and do not feed or touch the fish, even if your guide does.

Caution! Tidal currents here can be quite strong. Weak swimmers and children may tire quickly swimming against the current. Over the years, a couple of snorkelers were swept out to sea and perished. Ask your guide about the strength of the current at the time you are there, and let the guide know if you are not a good swimmer or have any disability. Don't be shy about accepting a life jacket.

Shark-Ray Alley is a shallow cut to the south of Hol Chan where nurse sharks and sting rays congregate. Guides sometimes chum to attract the sharks, and you can jump in and swim with them. It's not half as scary as it sounds, and most of the people who come on the snorkel boats do get in the water here.

At Mexico Rocks, off North Ambergris opposite a former coconut plantation, you may not see as many fish as at Hol Chan, but the coral is beautiful. Also, this area is protected from ocean swells and currents, so it makes for easier snorkeling. It is a good place for novice snorkelers. Depth is only about 5 to 12 feet, so you can see everything up close, and if necessary you can usually find a place to stand with your head above water. Water viz is about the same as at Hol Chan, 50 feet or more.

Day snorkel trips to Hol Chan cost around US$30 to $40 per adult, plus a US$10 park fee, and to Mexico Rocks US$35 to $50. These prices may include snorkel mask and fin rental and a guide who will go into the water with you and point out the sights. Kids under about age 12 go for half price.

These snorkeling trips usually last two to three hours. Typically, snorkel boats go out once in the morning and once in the afternoon, more frequently during busy periods. A couple of dozen dive and snorkel operators offer snorkel trips. It is difficult to recommend one over another, as the quality of the experience depends on who is your guide on a particular trip and also the weather and sea conditions. However, see the list of recommended dive shops in the dive section below.   Note that boats cannot always go out, due to wind and weather conditions. When there's a strong wind or during "Northers" in the late fall and early winter, snorkeling is unpleasant at best and could be dangerous.

Night snorkeling trips also are available, at around US$40 to $60 per person. Night snorkelers may see lobster, eels, octopus and other creatures.

For those who don't want to get in the water, there are glass-bottom boats You'll pay about US$45 per person plus the park fee. One glass-bottom boat is *Reef Runner* (www.ambergriscaye.com/reefrunner/, tel. 501-226-2180).

Catamarans and other vessels based in San Pedro visit some of Belize's other cayes and atolls, on longer trips for snorkeling and picnics. You typically pay US$40 to $75 for these trips, plus the $10 park fee if you go to Hol Chan, depending on the length of the trip, where you go and whether lunch and drinks are included. Many visitors say they really enjoy the day snorkel trips with a beach barbecue, featuring fresh-caught fish. *(See Day Trips and Tours below.)*

It's a long way to go for snorkeling, but Belize's atolls offer good snorkeling in shallow water around patch reefs. Day snorkel trips to Lighthouse or Turneffe atolls run about US$150 to $185, plus a US$40 park fee for Lighthouse, including lunch and snacks.

DIVING: LOCAL AND AROUND ATOLLS

Some **resort owners in San Pedro would have you believe the diving around Ambergris Caye is among the best in the Caribbean. It is not.** The diving immediately around Ambergris Caye is easily accessible and enjoyable but few would call it world-class. Outside the Hol Chan area, heavy fishing has reduced the size and quantity of fish. You won't see the huge lobster or megagroupers here that you do around Cozumel, which has for many years controlled fishing and lobstering. There is also some environmental degradation to the reef due to heavy use, although permanent mooring buoys at some sites have reduced anchor damage. Coral bleaching, caused by rising temperatures in the sea, likely associated with global warming, also has turned some of the colorful reef areas monochromatic.

Still, novice or recreational divers will enjoy the shallow dives and get to see a good variety of sea life and coral. Those willing to make a larger investment in time and money can use San Pedro as a base for day trips to distant cayes and atolls, which definitely do offer some of the best diving in all of the Caribbean. Diving around the atolls is mostly wall diving, while diving around Ambergris is spur-and-groove with some deep canyons, swim throughs and reef cuts.

Wave action from Hurricanes Mitch and Keith, and in 2001 from Tropical Storm Chantal and Hurricane Iris, did only limited damage to dive sites around Ambergris Caye. The storms destroyed some fragile coral, such as elk horn and seafans, especially near the water surface, and caused temporary loss of pigmentation in hard coral, but they scoured out green algae and cleaned out sand.

One of the good things about Ambergris Caye, in the eyes of many, is that it does not cater only to divers. Indeed, the majority of visitors to the island now are not divers, and this means that those who don't dive will not feel they are just extra

69

baggage on a dive machine. Ambergris Caye offers a good mix of dive and non-dive activities. Those who wish to do nothing but dive, eat, sleep, and dive may be better off choosing a dive lodge on one of the remote atolls or a live-aboard dive boat.

Among the **popular dive sites around Ambergris Caye are Hol Chan Cut, Tackle Box Canyon, Punta Arena Canyons, Tres Cocos and Basil Jones Canyons.**

Two-tank dives around Ambergris Caye typically go for US$65 to $75. One-tank dives are about US$20 less; three-tank dives about US$25 more. Rates usually include tanks, weights and belts. Other equipment is extra; US$20 to $25 is about average for a full set of gear. Off-season rates sometimes go down a little, typically 10 to 15%, but some shops keep the same rates year-round. (Note: Since mid-2006, prices for diving, snorkeling and most other tourist services include the 10% Goods and Services Tax; some operators may quote a price without GST and add it on, though government rules prohibit this.)

Those looking for even better diving likely will consider diving one of Belize's atolls. These are Pacific-style atolls with coral islands surrounding a fairly shallow lagoon. Only four true atolls exist in the Western Hemisphere; three of them are off Belize. **Belize's three atolls are Turneffe, Lighthouse and Glover's.** The fourth is off the coast of Mexico's Yucatán in the Chinchorra Banks. Turneffe and Lighthouse are closest to Ambergris Caye and are practical day trips.

For the more-serious diver, there is variety enough here to make for many weeks of diving. Visibility is terrific, often 150 feet or more. While many of the sites are best for intermediate and advanced divers, some are suitable for novice divers.

From San Pedro, expect to pay about US$165 to $225 for a day trip to Lighthouse or Turneffe, depending on the number of dives. Lunch and bottled water and soft drinks are usually included. At Lighthouse, there is an additional US$40 marine reserve fee.

Lighthouse Reef is about 60 miles east of Belize City. Lighthouse is home to Half Moon Caye Natural Monument, comprising about 15 square miles of atoll plus another 15 square miles of surrounding waters. Protected as a marine reserve since 1981, Lighthouse teems with birds, including a nesting colony of rare red-footed boobies. Under water life is also rich here, with dolphins and other creatures.

A typical trip to Lighthouse takes one and a half hours to two hours each way, includes three dives, a snorkel stop, a picnic lunch at Half Moon Caye, snacks and soft drinks. It costs about US$250 per person, including the marine reserve fee. Note that occasionally dive trips are canceled if not enough divers sign up for a specific trip. Boats to Lighthouse leave early, usually around 6 or 6:30 a.m., returning by about 6 p.m.

At Lighthouse also is the Blue Hole, a limestone sinkhole up to 1,000 feet across and more than 400 feet deep, made famous by Jacques Cousteau. The underwater cenote has stalactites and other natural formations, and sharks often frequent the deep waters.   Divers usually report that while the Blue Hole is worth doing once, it is more spectacular when seen from the air then from underwater. The Blue Hole is usually included as one of the three dives on a trip to Lighthouse.

While diving the Blue Hole is generally safe, its depths make diving here trickier than at some other sites. About five divers have died in the Blue Hole over the past 25 years.

The Turneffe Islands are about 20 miles east of Belize City. This is the largest atoll and the closest to the mainland. It differs somewhat from the other two atolls in that most of the islands here are densely covered in mangroves, especially on the west side. Black Beauty, Myrtle's Turtle and Mauger Caye (north of the atoll, with a lighthouse) are among the popular dive sites here. Mauger is known for its sharks. Boats to

Turneffe from San Pedro leave early, usually around 6:30 to 7 a.m., returning by around 6 p.m. Expect to pay around US$175 to $185 for an all-day, three-tank dive trip to Turneffe.

Glover's Reef is about 30 miles east of Dangriga. The perimeter of the atoll has elk horn coral forests. Here and in a deeper sandy area is a great variety of fish and sea life, including many sharks. Shark Point, northeast of North Caye with its lighthouse, is well-known for hammerhead and tiger sharks. Glover's is a little too far to go for a day-trip from Ambergris Caye. Dangriga, Hopkins and Placencia are common jumping off points for Glover's.

San Pedro has the country's only hyperbaric chamber. It's located near the airstrip. Most dive shops ask for a small donation with each tank fill which goes toward funding the chamber.

For those who don't dive but would like to, several Ambergris Caye dive shops offer dive courses and training. A resort course costs about US$150 to $175. This includes classroom training, practice in a pool or in the water, and an actual dive, usually at Hol Chan. Complete open water certification runs US$450 to $475 and requires four days. For those who have completed classroom instruction elsewhere, the two-day open water training is about US$300.

Water temperatures around Ambergris Caye hover in the low 80s year-round, typically rising to about 83 or 84 degrees in late summer and sometimes dipping into the high 70s in January and February. At around 100 feet in the Blue Hole the water temp is around 76 degrees year-round. Most divers feel comfortable in a "shortie" or less.

Shore diving? There is none on Ambergris Caye, though on the far north of the island a few people do clamber in the water and swim out to the reef.

Jellyfish are not usually a big problem in Belize waters. Late spring and summer is when they are most likely to be around. In the winter and early spring few jellyfish are seen. There are no deadly jellyfish in Caribbean waters.

The larva stage of jellyfish, called **"pica pica"** (which means itchy-itchy in Spanish) or more colorfully "sea lice," can cause skin irritation, welts that itch for a day or two. You may run into them from around March to early June. They affect mostly snorkelers or swimmers, as they occur near the surface. Old sea hands recommend spreading petroleum jelly over exposed skin before going into the water, or spraying affected areas with any alcohol-based household cleaner, which seems to stop the itching. Cortisone cream also works.

DIVE SHOPS

Dive operations and their principals come and go, so it's always a good idea to check locally for current recommendations, but here are some of the Ambergris Caye dive shops recommended by knowledgeable divers. It is not an exhaustive list. Note that many dive shops also offer snorkel trips, fishing trips and tours.

Amigos del Mar Dive Shop, tel. 501-226-2706, fax 226-2648, www.amigosdive.com. This PADI shop, on a pier near the center of San Pedro Town, is probably the most consistently recommended dive operation on the island.

Ecologic Divers, tel. 501-226-4118, www.ecologicdivers.com. Located on a 300-ft. pier at the north end of San Pedro, Ecologic Divers is a PADI shop. Along with other dive trips, it offers an early morning dive that get you back to town by around 9 a.m. Ecologic also has a tour office and gear shop at the south end of town, next to Wine DeVine.

Fantasea Scuba School and Sports Center, tel. 501-226-2576, www.ambergriscaye.com/fantasea/index.html.   This PADI facility at Victoria House offers a variety of instruction and diving options.

Patojo's Scuba Center, tel. 501-226-2283, fax 226-3797, www.ambergriscaye.com/tides/dive.html. This PADI shop at The Tides hotel just north of town is one of the few operations on the island owned and run by a Belizean by birth, in this case Elmer "Patojo" Paz.

ProTech Belize Dive Centre, tel. 501-226-3008 or 866-703-9677, www.protechdive.com.   This PADI shop has garnered many excellent reviews.

Ramon's Village, tel. 800-624-4215 or 501-226-2071, fax 226-2214, www.ramons.com.   Ramon's, a PADI Gold Palm facility, is a large dive operation with seven boats ranging from 24 to 42 feet in length. Ramon's handles Nitrox.

White Sands Dive Shop, tel. 501-226-2405, www.scuba-lessonsbelize.com, is run by veteran divemaster Elbert Greer. It's now located at Las Terazzas on North Ambergris.

FISHING: FLATS, REEF, DEEP SEA, SHORE

Southern Belize and several of the remote cayes are better known centers for serious gamefishing, but the waters around Ambergris Caye also offer a great variety of saltwater fishing. The lagoons and flats on the back side of Ambergris hold bone-fish, permit and barracuda. The river mouths and estuaries are home to snook, jacks and tarpon. Grouper, jacks, snapper and other fish hang out around the barrier reef. The deep blue waters beyond the reef contain marlin, sailfish and other big fish. Many fish, including bone fish and tarpon, can be caught year-round. Within 15 minutes of leaving the dock, you can be fishing in tidal flats or in blue water hundreds of feet deep, and you can even catch fish from the beach or a dock. Like Placencia, Ambergris Caye has many experienced fishing guides.

Size of fish: Typical sizes caught around Ambergris Caye: tarpon, up to 100 pounds in the lagoon but larger elsewhere; bonefish, 2 to 8 pounds; permit, 3 to 30 pounds;   barracuda, 3 to 25 pounds; snook, mostly 5 to 10 pounds.

Licenses: You now need a license for salt-water fishing in Belize. If you plan to fish in Belize, whether around the cayes or even from a pier on the mainland, you now need a saltwater fishing license. Costs are US$10 per day, US$25 per week or US$50 per year. As of this writing, the rules and regulations on licenses are unclear (as are many things in Belize), but your fishing guide or hotel can assist in getting you a license, or, failing that, contact **Belize Coastal Zone Management** in Belize City (www.coastalzonebelize.org, tel. 501-223-0719). In a few marine reserve areas, such as Port Honduras Marine Reserve in southern Belize, a daily fee also is charged for fishing.

Shore, beach and dock fishing: Not many people, locals or visitors, fish from shore on Ambergris, but that doesn't mean you can't do it. It's certainly cheap entertainment, and you can catch all types of fish, from barracuda to snapper, jacks and grouper. Light tackle with small spinners and grubs can be used for any type of fish. For the best shore fishing, you'll want to get away from the developed areas and head north or south. One easily accessible fishing area begins about one-half mile north of the bridge, on the back (west) side. Here you have a good shot at red snapper and cuda, among other fish. You can also catch bonefish here or anywhere in the shallow flats on the back side. Watch out for the occasional croc. Late in the afternoon is a good time to fish from the docks, especially south of town.

Bait and tackle: For fly fishing, a stiff 8 or 9 weight rod will work for most situations. For spin fishing, a long medium-action rod for bonefish and permit and a stiff heavy-action rod for tarpon and large reef species are all you need. Bait – sardines are best – can be bought at small bait shops — ask locally. El Pescador has a fly fishing shop.

What to do with your fish: If you catch eating fish and aren't staying in condo or house with kitchen, many restaurants in San Pedro will clean and cook them for you for around US$5 per person. It helps if you'll give the restaurant a little extra fish that they can serve to regular customers.

Spearfishing: Spearfishing by non-citizens is legal only if you are doing it with mask, fins and snorkel, using Hawaiian sling-type gear. It is illegal to spearfish with scuba equipment. You also cannot spearfish in a marine reserve or national park.

When fish are biting:
Tarpon: Around all year, but the best tarpon fishing is April – August
Bonefish: Present all year but peak from April – October
Permit: Best fishing is April – August
King mackerel: April – June
Marlin and sailfish: Anytime, but best months are March – June
Snapper: Anytime
Grouper: December – February
Barracuda: All months
Marlin: All months
Wahoo: Winter best

Cost: Cost for charters depends on the type of fishing (reef, deep sea, or bone and tarpon), the size of the boat, number of anglers, time of year and current bank balance of the captain, but expect to pay around US$200 to $350 for a full day's fishing trip, including guide, bait and tackle, and ice. This is for one or two people. You may find a guide for less but you get what you pay for.

Tipping: US$20 to $25 a day per boat (one or two anglers) is common.

Fishing guides: Ask locally for current information on fishing guides. **Rubie's Hotel** is a good place to start. **El Pescador** on North Ambergris is a small hotel that specializes in fishing pack-ages. Among local fishing guides recommended by knowledge-able anglers are:
Omar Arceo, tel. 501-226-2410

George and Roberto Bradley, Victoria House, tel. 501-226-2179
Gil Gonzalez, tel. 501-226-2118
Eloy Gonzalez, tel. 501-226-2337 (nephew of Gil)
Carlos Marin and Nesto Gomez, El Pescador (tel. 501-226-2398)
Luis Caliz, tel. 501-226-2785
Severo Guerrero, tel. 501-226-2324,
Ramon Guerrero, tel. 501-226-2325

Steve DeMaio can book most guides for you. Check his web site, www.fishingsanpedro.com.

SHOPPING

Most of the shopping on the island, such as it is, is on Barrier Reef Drive. Our philosophy about shopping is that those who like it will quickly sniff out the best places, without anyone, especially someone who hates to shop, telling them where to find the good stuff and the bargains. We'll make suggestions only about a few items:

For cigars: Several small shops in town sell what are purport-ed to be Cuban cigars, for US$6 to $15 each. **Travellers** on Pescador Drive (tel. 501-226-2020) has a humidor. **Rum, Cigar & Coffee Shop** (Pescador Drive, tel. 501-226-2020) makes and sells Belizean cigars (US$3 to $10 each).

For art: **Belizean Arts** (tel. 501-226-2638) at Fido's Courtyard has interesting stuff from Belize and elsewhere in Central America.

For wine: **Wine DeVine** (7 Tarpon St., tel. 501-226-3430) and **Premium Wine & Spirits** (Barrier Reef Drive at SunBreeze Suites).

ALL ABOUT HOTELS AND RESORTS ON AMBERGRIS CAYE

Here's the skinny on where to stay and how to stretch your lodging dollars.

WHERE TO STAY: TOWN? NORTH? SOUTH?

Probably the biggest decision you'll make about Ambergris Caye is where to stay. We're not talking about a specific hotel but about the general area. The area you choose will determine to a great degree the experience you have on the island. You have four basic options:

1) in the town of San Pedro

2) just to the south of San Pedro near the airstrip, within walking distance of town

3) on the south end, beyond easy walking distance to town
4) on the north end of the island above the channel.

There is no one "best" place to stay. Each of these four areas has advantages and disadvantages. Which area you choose depends on what you want from your vacation. If you're looking for privacy and the feeling of being away from it all, consider the south end or the north end of the island. If you prefer easy access to restaurants, nightlife, shops and other activities, you'll likely be happier in San Pedro town or nearby. There's little or no advantage to any one area in terms of beaches, although the beaches in town tend to be more crowded with boats than those outside of town.

HEART OF TOWN: Hotels in the town of San Pedro, with a few notable exceptions, are older spots, among them the original tourist hotels on the island. They are, again with a few exceptions, less expensive digs. If you're looking to save a buck or two, this may be the place for you. You also will be right in the heart of things, no more than a few sandy blocks from some of the best restaurants, bars, shops and dive operations on the island. Party animals will want to stay here or just the south of town. Accommodations here include **Rubie's, Holiday Hotel, Spindrift, Lily's, Martha's, San Pedrano, Mayan Princess, Hotel del Rio** and **The Tides**. More expensive options in town include **The Phoenix** and **SunBreeze Suites.**

AIRSTRIP SOUTH: If you want a larger variety of moderate and upscale lodging but still want to be within walking distance of the attractions of San Pedro Town, think about staying at the south edge of town and the area just to the south of town. The San Pedro airstrip is here, but you should have few or no problems with airport noise, since the planes are small one- and two-engine prop jobs, and there are no flights after dark. This is a good compromise between the activity of town and the remoteness of the north end and far south end. Among the hotels here are **SunBreeze, The Palms, Belizean Reef Suites, Ramon's Village, Steve & Becky's Cute Little Hotel,**

Exotic Caye, Coconuts, Coral Bay Villas, Caribbean Villas, Belize Yacht Club and **Changes in Latitudes.**

SOUTH END: Although most of this area is beyond a quick walk to town, this a major growth area for tourism on the island. Some of the nicer upmarket hotels are located here, and more are on the way. An increasing number of restaurants and amenities also are located here. At the far end, you're two to three miles from San Pedro, so for visits to town you'll need to rent a golf cart (US$60 or $65 for 24 hours), ride a bike (some hotels offer them free to guests), take a taxi (about US$5 to town) or take a hotel shuttle, if available. Among the choices here are **Villas at Banyan Bay, Grand Colony, Banana Beach, Mata Rocks, Royal Palm, Victoria House, Caribe Island Resort, Royal Caribbean, Sunset Beach** and **Pelican Reef Villas.**

NORTH AMBERGRIS: By all accounts, the area north of "the River" – a narrow channel of water separating the south and north ends of the island – is where much of Ambergris Caye's growth will occur over the next decade or two. Houses, hotels, and even a restaurant or two are going up here. At present, though, access is limited by the fact that there are only two ways to get to the north end: One is by boat, usually a water taxi, either scheduled or on-demand. The other is via a bridge, new in early 2006, open only to pedestrians, bikes and golf carts, and then via a hike or ride on a narrow path to the various resorts and villas. Bring plenty of bug spray for use when you're away from the water. Crossing the bridge costs US$2.50 each way for a golf cart, US$1 for a pedestrian. Water taxis are US$5 to $20 per person for most destinations.

Accommodations on the north end include **Cocotel Inn, Ak'Bol, Grand Caribe, El Pescador, Capricorn, Captain Morgan's, Belizean Shores, Coco Beach, Seascape Villas, Las Terrazas, Azul Resort, Mata Chica, Xamen Ek, La Perla del Caribe, Portofino, Costa Maya, Blue Reef, Salamander, Sueño del Mar** and **Tranquility Bay.**

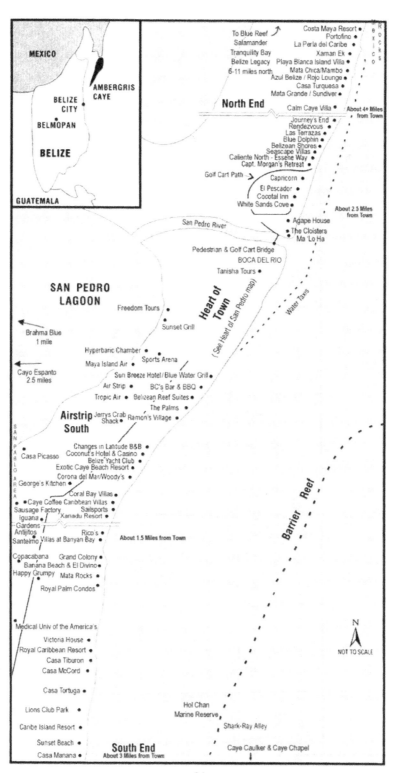

MEXICO

AMBERGRIS CAYE

BELIZE CITY

BELMOPAN

BELIZE

GUATEMALA

M e x i c o   R O C K S

To Blue Reef
Salamander
Tranquility Bay
Belize Legacy
6-11 miles north

Costa Maya Resort •
Portofino •
La Perla del Caribe •
Xaman Ek •
Playa Blanca Island Villa •
Mata Chica/Mambo •
Azul Belize / Rojo Lounge •
Casa Turquesa •
Mata Grande / Sundiver •

North End

Calm Caye Villa •

About 4+ Miles from Town

Journey's End •
Rendezvous •
Las Terrazas •
Blue Dolphin •
Belizean Shores •
Seascape Villas •
Caliente North - Essene Way •
Capt. Morgan's Retreat •

Golf Cart Path →

Capricorn •
El Pescador •
Cocotal Inn •
White Sands Cove •

About 2.5 Miles from Town

San Pedro River

• Agape House
• The Cloisters
Ma 'Lo Ha

Pedestrian & Golf Cart Bridge
BOCA DEL RIO

Tanisha Tours •

SAN PEDRO LAGOON

Heart of Town
(See Heart of San Pedro map)

Freedom Tours •

Water Taxis

← Brahma Blue
1 mile

Sunset Grill •

← Cayo Espanto
2.5 miles

Hyperbaric Chamber •
Sports Arena •
Maya Island Air •
Sun Breeze Hotel / Blue Water Grill •
Air Strip • BC's Bar & BBQ •
Tropic Air • Belizean Reef Suites •
The Palms •
Jerrys Crab Shack Ramon's Village •

Airstrip South

S A N   P A B L O   A R E A

Changes in Latitude B&B •
Coconut's Hotel & Casino •
Belize Yacht Club •
Exotic Caye Beach Resort •
Corona del Mar/Woody's •
George's Kitchen •
Casa Picasso •
Coral Bay Villas •
• Caye Coffee Caribbean Villas
Sausage Factory Sailsports •
Iguana •
Gardens
Antijitos
Santelmo Villas at Banyan Bay •

Rico's •

About 1.5 Miles from Town

Copacabana • Grand Colony •
Banana Beach & El Divino •
Happy Grumpy Mata Rocks •

Royal Palm Condos •

Barrier Reef

• Medical Univ of the America's

Victoria House •
Royal Caribbean Resort •
Casa Tiburon •
Casa McCord •

Casa Tortuga •

N

NOT TO SCALE

Lions Club Park •

Caribe Island Resort •

Hol Chan
Marine Reserve

Sunset Beach •
Casa Manana •

South End
About 3 Miles from Town

Shark-Ray Alley

Caye Caulker & Caye Chapel
↓

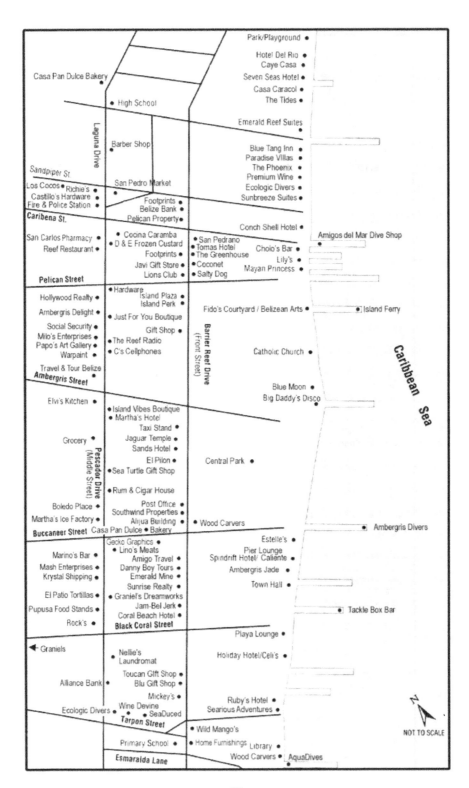

Park/Playground •

Hotel Del Rio •
Caye Casa •
Seven Seas Hotel •
Casa Caracol •
The Tides •

Casa Pan Dulce Bakery •

Emerald Reef Suites •

• High School

Laguna Drive

Blue Tang Inn •
Paradise Villas •
The Phoenix •
Premium Wine •
Ecologic Divers •
Sunbreeze Suites •

• Barber Shop

Sandpiper St

Los Cocos • Richie's •
Castillo's Hardware •
Fire & Police Station •

San Pedro Market

Footprints •
Belize Bank •
Pelican Property •

Caribena St.

Conch Shell Hotel •

Amigos del Mar Dive Shop

San Carlos Pharmacy •
Reef Restaurant •

• Cocina Caramba
• D & E Frozen Custard
Footprints •
Javi Gift Store •
Lions Club •

• San Pedrano
• Tomas Hotel
• The Greenhouse
• Coconet
• Salty Dog

Cholo's Bar •
Lily's •
Mayan Princess •

Pelican Street

Hollywood Realty •

• Hardware
Island Plaza
Island Perk •

Barrier Reef Drive (Front Street)

Fido's Courtyard / Belizean Arts •

• Island Ferry

Ambergris Delight •

• Just For You Boutique

Social Security •
Milo's Enterprises •
Papo's Art Gallery •
Warpaint •

Gift Shop •
• The Reef Radio
• C's Cellphones

Catholic Church •

Travel & Tour Belize •

Ambergris Street

Blue Moon •
Big Daddy's Disco •

Elvi's Kitchen •

• Island Vibes Boutique
• Martha's Hotel
Taxi Stand •
Jaguar Temple •
Sands Hotel •
El Pilon •
• Sea Turtle Gift Shop

Grocery •

Pescador Drive (Middle Street)

Central Park •

• Rum & Cigar House

Boledo Place •
Martha's Ice Factory •

Post Office •
Southwind Properties •
Alijua Building •

• Wood Carvers

Buccaneer Street   Casa Pan Dulce • Bakery

Ambergris Divers

Gecko Graphics •
• Lino's Meats
Amigo Travel •
Danny Boy Tours •
Emerald Mine •
Sunrise Realty •
• Graniel's Dreamworks
Jam-Bel Jerk •
Coral Beach Hotel •

Estelle's •
Pier Lounge •
Spindrift Hotel/ Caliente •
Ambergris Jade •
Town Hall •

Marino's Bar •
Mash Enterprises •
Krystal Shipping •

El Patio Tortillas •

Pupusa Food Stands •

Rock's •

Black Coral Street

Tackle Box Bar

Playa Lounge •

← Graniels

Nellie's
Laundromat •

Holiday Hotel/Celi's •

Alliance Bank •

Toucan Gift Shop •
Blu Gift Shop •

Mickey's •
Wine Devine •
• SeaDuced

Ruby's Hotel •
Searious Adventures •

Ecologic Divers •

Tarpon Street

• Wild Mango's

Primary School •

• Home Furnishings Library •
Wood Carvers • • AquaDives

Esmaralda Lane

Caribbean Sea

N

NOT TO SCALE

82

Not on Ambergris but close by, off the back side of the island, is **Cayo Espanto** and on Caye Chapel, the **Caye Chapel Island Resort.**

Here are approximate distances, in driving miles, of hotels and resorts from Central Park in San Pedro Town, roughly the center of town. Your mileage may vary.

SOUTH END

Pelican Reef	2.8 miles south
Miramar Villas	2.5 miles south
Sunset Beach Resort	2.5 miles south
Royal Caribbean Resort	1.9 miles south
Victoria House	1.8 miles south
Mata Rocks	1.4 miles south
Banana Beach Resort	1.4 miles south
Grand Colony	1.3 miles south
The Villas at Banyan Bay	1.2 miles south

AIRSTRIP SOUTH

Xanadu	1 mile south
Caribbean Villas	1 mile south
Coral Bay Villas	1 mile south
Coconuts Caribbean	.9 miles south
Corona del Mar	.9 miles south
Exotic Caye Beach Resort	.8 miles south
Belize Yatch Club	.7 miles south
Changes in Latitudes	.6 miles south
Pedro's Backpacker's Inn	.6 miles south
Ramon's Village	.4 miles south
Steve & Becky's	.4 miles south
The Palms	.4 miles south
Belizean Reef Suites	.3 miles south
Sunbreeze Hotel	.3 miles south

IN TOWN

Ruby's	.2 miles south
Holiday Hotel	.2 miles south

Coral Beach Hotel	.2 miles south
Spendrift Hotel	.1 miles south
Martha's Hotel	.1 miles south
Mayan Princess	.0 miles
Hotel SanPedrano	.0 miles
Lily's	.0 miles
Conch Shell	.1 miles north
SeaBreeze Suites	.1 miles north
The Phoenix	.3 miles north
Paradise Villas	.3 miles north
Blue Tang Inn	.4 miles north
The Tides Beach Resort	.5 miles north
Seven Seas	.6 miles north
Hotel del Rio	.7 miles north

NORTH AMBERGRIS

Reef Village	1.4 miles north
The Cloisters	1.5 miles north
Ak'Bol	2.0 miles north
Grand Caribe	2.5 miles north
Cocotal Inn	2.5 miles north
El Pescador Lodge	2.9 miles north
Capricorn Resort	3.0 miles north
Capt. Morgan's Retreat	3.1 miles north
Coco Beach	3.1 miles north
Seascape Villas	3.2 miles north
Belizean Shores	3.3 miles north
Las Terrazas	3.8 miles north
Azul Resort	5.1 miles north
Mata Chica	5.2 miles north
Xaman Ek	5.6 miles north
Portofino Resort	6.0 miles north
Costa Maya Reef Resort	6.7 miles north
Blue Reef	8.1 miles north
Sueño del Mar	11.5 miles north
Tranquility Bay	12.0 miles north

HOW TO GET THE BEST HOTEL RATES

Ambergris Caye hotel rates are not cheap, averaging near US$200 double in high season, although rooms are available for under US$25, and you can pay US$500 or more a night.   Rates in San Pedro, however, compare favorably with those in most resort areas of Mexico and Costa Rica and generally are far less than on Caribbean islands such as St. Maarten/St. Martin, Anguilla or St. Thomas.

There are several things you can do to enjoy lower prices. The most obvious is simply to go off-season, when most hotels drop rates 20 to 40%. Exact dates vary from hotel to hotel, but the low season generally starts just after Easter and runs until about mid-November. The island has more than 50 hotels, with additional ones under construction. Occupancy rates on the island average less than 50%, so there are normally rooms available even in high season. Easter and Christmas/New Years are usually almost fully booked.

With most hotels having excess capacity, particularly in June, September and October and to a lesser degree also in the other off-season months, discounts of several types are available. In the off-season, many hotels have "walk-in" rates. These rates, typically 15 to 20% off the already discounted summer rates, can be real values. You can sometimes get the walk-in rate on advance direct bookings, or at least get a discount off the published rate.

Many hotels on Ambergris Caye also post special discounted rates for September and October, the two slowest months of the year for tourism.

Many hotels also offer sizable discounts for stays of a week or longer, or have a value package such as "stay seven nights/pay for five." Frequently, hotels offer discounts for Internet or other direct bookings, saving them travel agent or wholesaler commissions. These direct booking discounts usually range from 10 to 20%, and occasionally are as much as 30%.

When booking, always ask, "Is that your best rate?" or "Do you have a lower rate?" or "That's a little more than I was hoping to pay – is there a way I can get a better rate?" Keep probing to find out if you're getting the best price.

Most hotels require a deposit to hold reservations, usually non-refundable or only partially refundable.

Nearly all hotels on the island accept **Visa** and **MasterCard**. Some accept **American Express.** Only a few accept **Discover.** If credit cards are not accepted, this is noted in the hotel reviews. Some hotels still surcharge credit cards by 5% or so, but this practice happily is declining.

OCCUPANCY RATES

Hotels in Belize generally do not enjoy high annual occupancy rates. In recent years, the country-wide occupancy rate has been in the low 40% range. The last year for which statistics from the Belize Tourism Board are available, 2008, it was 41.1%. This is at least 20 percentage points lower than annual occupancy rates in the U.S., Europe and the main Caribbean.

(Note that a 2006 Inter-American Development Bank study concluded that the BTB methodology overstated actual occupancy rates. The authors determined country-wide occupancy rates were actually around 27%. On the other hand, some in tourism in Belize believe that some hotel owners actually report lower occupancies than they enjoy, as a way of avoiding taxes.)

Ambergris Caye enjoys the highest hotel occupancy rate of any area of Belize, with occupancy rates in the mid-40s percent range. Some of the most popular properties have occupancy rates of over 70%, and near 100% at the height of the season. Many properties are virtually completely booked at Christmas, New Years, Easter and at times during the high season, especially March, the busiest month of the year for tourism in Belize.

Caye Caulker's hotel occupancy rate in for the last year reported, 2008, was 40%, according to the BTB, and offshore islands had an occupancy rate of 29.1%.

Occupancy rate by area, 2008:

Belize District	42.3%
Ambergris Caye	44.3%
Caye Caulker	40.0%
Cayo	39.4%
Corozal	19.7%
Orange Walk	38.6%
Stann Creek	43.6%
Placencia	39.2%
Toledo	27.5%
Other Islands	29.1%

LODGING TYPES

You have several different types of lodging from which to choose on Ambergris Caye:

Condotels: These are condominiums run like a hotel. Units are individually owned and rented to visitors by on-site management that typical takes 40 to 60% of the gross. They have most of the same amenities as a regular hotel, except usually not a restaurant. Most condotels on Ambergris Caye are not the large sprawling condo complexes found in Florida or Hawaii. They are small, only two to four stories high, with up to a few dozen units. Typically they have a mix of one- and two-bedroom units; a few have three-bedroom suites. The advantage of a condotel is that you get a lot more space, including a kitchen, for a price not much more than for a regular hotel. The drawback is that most condotels do not offer the range of services of a hotel, such as room service. Condotels range in price from under US$100 to over US$500 a night. Among the condotels on Ambergris Caye are **Villas at Banyan Bay, Belizean Shores, Coral Bay Villas, Mayan Princess, Grand Colony, Grand Caribe, Pelican Reef** and **Xanadu.**

Beachside cabañas and cottages: These come in two flavors – thatch and not. Thatch cabañas have thatch roofs and palapa-style walls, usually over concrete block or wood frames. Among resorts with thatch cabañas (in some cases, only some units are thatch) are **Salamander Hideaway, Portofino, Captain Morgan's, Hotel del Rio, Ak' Bol, Ramon's Village, Exotic Caye, Xanadu** and **Victoria House.** Other properties have more traditional wood-frame or concrete cottages or cabins.   Beachside cabañas are available from around US$75 to more than US$600 a night.

Hotels: Nearly all hotels on the island are personality inns. Most are small, under 30 rooms. Hotels come in all price ranges, from US$15 to over US$400 a night. Nearly all the hotels, except for a few budget places, are on the water.

Privately owned houses for vacation rental: Dozens of private homes and villas are available on Ambergris Caye for weekly rental. Rates start at around US$700 a week and go up to US$6,000 or more.

Longer-term rentals: Monthly rentals of houses and apartments are available, starting at around US$300 for a small apartment, though most rentals are US$500 to $1,000 and up. The best way to find a rental is to ask around in person.

CAMPING

There are currently no campgrounds on Ambergris Caye, and camping, unless on your own land or on other private land with permission, is prohibited. Caye Caulker has a small private campground, and primitive camping is available on some outlying cayes, including Half Moon Caye.

Your Lodging Choices

These hotel reviews are candid and are not influenced by advertising (we accept none) or by comps. Keep in mind that hotel reviews, like movie reviews, are matters of opinion. Your mileage may vary.

Also, keep in mind that things change – rates, amenities, management. We routinely check with properties for current and projected rates. Note that rates for the Christmas, New Year's and Easter holidays may be higher than those shown here, and minimum stays may be required for those prime holiday periods.

HOTEL STAR RATINGS

We've given hotels and resorts on the island star ratings ranging from one to five stars, with pluses (+) or minuses (-) possible. Keep in mind that, although there is no direct correlation between the price of a hotel room and the hotel's star rating, three- to five-star hotels are likely to be considerably more expensive than one- or two-star properties. Some travelers may be willing to accept a lower level of amenities and services in exchange for a lower price, or they may even prefer staying in inexpensive lodging to better appreciate the local culture.

Our ratings are necessarily subjective, but they are based in most cases on multiple visits over many years and often on personal stays at the properties. If you disagree with our ratings, please let us know.

★★★★★   One of the top hotels in the entire Caribbean, with strong management, excellent service, striking location and/or exceptional facilities and wide selection of amenities such as swimming pool, spa or sports offerings.

★★★★ One of the best hotels in Belize, with a dependably high level of hospitality and in most cases with amenities such as swimming pool or sports facilities.

★★★   Excellent accommodations, with above-average amenities, service and hospitality.

★★   Good accommodations and often a very good value.

★   Functional, clean accommodations, meeting basic needs, and often a good value.

SAN PEDRO TOWN

(Listed from the north to south. The hotels just north of town, including Hotel Del Rio, Seven Seas and The Tides, are about a 10 minute walk along the beach to town.)

★★ **Hotel Del Rio.** Boca Del Rio Drive, tel./fax 501-226-2286; www.ambergriscaye.com/hoteldelrio/index.html.   At this small seafront operation, you have the choice of a big cabaña, a small cabaña, less-expensive rooms in a Mexican-style building and even more modest rooms in a guesthouse. This is not a fancy resort, but it has personality some other places lack. In-season doubles are US$50 to $145, off-season US$40 to $105, plus 9% tax. Bottom line: Worth considering if you're watching your pennies and want a bit of thatch ambiance.

★★+ **Seven Seas Resort.** Boca Del Rio Drive, tel. 501-226-2382, or toll-free 866-438-1435; www.AmbergrisCaye.com/sevenseas/index.html.   This long-established beachfront property has gone through a variety of incarnations over the years, including timeshare, but it remains a good value, though not an upscale one, at the north edge of town, within walking distance of downtown restaurants. In a small cluster of three-story pink and white buildings you'll find air-conditioned one-bedroom suites with tile floors and Belizean-made furniture. There's a small pool and a pier. Free wireless. Rates for direct booking in-season: US$101-$115, off-season, US$88-$102. Bottom line: Rates for one-bedroom suites are hard to beat.

★★★ **The Tides Beach Resort.** Boca Del Rio Drive, tel. 501-226-2283, fax 226-3797; www.ambergriscaye.com/tides/. Owned and operated by San Pedranos Patojo and Sabrina Paz and with Patojo's Scuba Center on-site, this 12-unit hotel focuses on divers, and you'll often see wet suits and dive gear hanging over the balcony.   Though built just a few years ago, with its wood construction and balconied verandahs, this three-story hotel has a vaguely colonial era appearance. The rooms are modern enough, though, with fans and pleasant furnishings. The hotel also offers two and three-bedroom suites with kitchens. No restaurant, but several good ones are nearby, and there's a tiny beach bar and a pool. Off-season rates are US$85 with A/C, and US$125 (suites US$205) in-season. Plus tax. Dive packages also available. Bottom line: Good spot for divers.

★★★ **Blue Tang Inn.** tel. 866-881-1020 or 501-226-2326, fax 226-2358; www.bluetanginn.com. The 14 studio-type suites with kitchens in this three-story blue hotel have been remodeled and upgraded, and there's a new "cozy" swimming pool. (For those who aren't divers, a Blue Tang is a colorful tropical fish seen around the barrier reef.) Rates US$120 to $180 off-season, US$150 to $210 November through April, including continental breakfast. Bottom-line: Quality suites accommodation at north edge of town.

★★★★+ **The Phoenix.** Barrier Reef Dr.; tel. 501-226-3414; www.ambergriscaye.com/phoenix. This beachfront condo is at the north end of town, on the site of what used to be a retreat for Catholic nuns and later the location of the Paradise Hotel. The 30 condo units are of nice size. The two-bedroom, two-bath units are around 1600 sq. ft., with kitchens, broadband internet and all the upscale amenities. There are two swimming pools, and an upscale restaurant, Red Ginger. Rates start at US$325 for a beautiful one-bedroom suite plus tax in-season.

★★★ **Paradise Villas.** Barrier Reef Drive, San Pedro. Paradise Villas is an attractive low-rise condo colony at the north end of town. In the past, a complication was that the units were managed and rented by several different companies, plus several owners of one or two units. However, we're told this confusing situation is improving. If you want to stay at Paradise Villas, just contact the agents and see what's available and compare prices. Choose from either one- or two-bedroom condos. The two-bedroom units are not as big as some other two-bedroom suites at island condotels. Though units vary in furnishings and amenities such as whether the air conditioning is just in the bedroom or throughout the units, they are basically similar. There's an attractive seaside pool area, and a small artificial reef at the end of the pier (built by the condo owners) to attract fish for snorkeling. Rates vary among the different agents, but most are in the range of US$135 to $200 in-season and US$90 to $150 off-season. Paradisee Villas, tel. 877-331-9693 or 882-331-9693; www.belizevilla.com. Nellie Gomez Property Management, P. O. Box 143, Pescador Drive, San Pedro Town; tel. 501-226-2087, fax 226-2400; www.nelliesproperty.com. Tradewinds (this travel wholesaler manages 12 Paradise units and has a manager with an office across the street), tel. in the U.S. 800-451-7776, fax 414-258-5336, in Belize tel. 501-226-2822, fax 226-3746; www.tradewindsparadisevillas.com. Bottom line: Comfortable, if slightly confusing, condo colony.

★★ **Conch Shell.** Barrier Reef Drive, P.O. Box 43, San Pedro;

tel. 501-226-2062; e-mail conchshell@btl.net. This center-of-town, water-front two-story hotel, with its wood-frame construction, ceiling fans and linoleum floors, is an option for travelers who just want a clean, simple place to stay. Recently renovately. Rates around US$69 to $89 double mid-November to mid-April, plus tax, US$10 less the rest of the year. Free wireless available. Bottom line: One of the better budget choices in town.

★★ **Tio Pil's Place** (formerly **Lily's Hotel).** Barrier Reef Drive, San Pedro; tel. 501-226-2059, fax 226-2623; www.ambergriscaye.com/lilys/index.html. This family-run budget favorite has been around for more than 35 years, recently going upmarket a bit with air-conditioning and some remodeling. Regulars prefer the seafront rooms. Those on the second-floor have breezy verandahs with sea views, while the first-floor rooms are for the gregarious who like to gab with passersby. Rooms are smallish and simple, but all have fridges and comfortable beds. Doubles US$65 off-season, US$75 in-season., plus tax Bottom line: An old favorite budget hotel.

★ **San Pedrano.** Barrier Reef Drive, San Pedro; tel. 501-226-2054, fax 226-2093. Six-room budget spot near the water. Bottom line: For the budget-minded.

★★★ **Mayan Princess.** Barrier Reef Drive, San Pedro; tel. 800-850-4101 or 501-226-2778, fax 226-2784; www.mayan-princesshotel.com. This three-story, seafront condotel, painted a distinctive coral pink, has 23 large and attractive one-bedroom suites (king or queen beds) with air conditioning, kitchenettes, phones and cable TV. Rates are a good value at US$120 double off-season, US$145 in-season, plus hotel tax and 10% service. Some further discounts may be available at certain times. Dive packages and long-term rates available. Amigos del Mar dive shop is nearby. No pool, but each suite has a balcony with wonderful views of the sea, and the whole atmosphere here is comfortable and homey. Long-time managers Rusty and Sheila Nale have moved on to Toledo, where they own Tranquility Lodge. Bottom line: Convenient, comfortable in-town suites on the water at reasonable rates.

★ **Martha's.** Pescador Drive and Ambergris Street, P.O. Box 27, San Pedro; tel. 501-226-2053, fax 226-2589; www.AmbergrisCaye.com/marthas/index.html. In the middle of town, not on the water, but a good budget choice with 12 clean rooms in a three-story wood building. No air conditioning and no phones in rooms. Rates US$27.50 double off-season, US$35 in-season, including tax. Monthly rates available off-season. Bottom line: Definitely stretches your lodging dollar.

★★ **Spindrift.** Barrier Reef Drive, San Pedro; tel. 800-688-0161 or 501-226-2174, fax 226-2251; www.AmbergrisCaye.com/spin-drift/. This dominating three-story concrete hotel won't win any awards from *Architectural Digest,* but it is on the water in the center of town, with 22 rooms and 2 one-bedroom apartments. All but the cheapest rooms have air-conditioning. Caliente restaurant is on the first floor, and the Pier Lounge at the hotel hosts the "famous chicken drop" at which drinkers bet on where a chicken will poop. Doubles in-season US$53 to $110, apartment US$150, a little less off-season, all plus tax and 5% service. Bottom-line: In-town convenience and a good place if you like chickens.

★★ **Coral Beach Hotel.** Barrier Reef, Drive, (P.O. Box 16), San Pedro; tel. 501-226-2013, fax 226-2864; www.coralbeachhotel.com. The 19 rooms at this long-estab-lished in-town spot, located on the west side of Barrier Reef Drive (not on the sea), are mostly small and basic, but all have fans and some have air-conditioning. The building has been upgraded a bit. Jam-Bel Jerk Pit restaurant is on the first floor. Rates US$46 double with fan, US$57 with A/C off-season, about US$57-$69 in-season. Bottom line: Another choice for the budget-minded.

★★★ **Holiday Hotel.** Barrier Reef Drive, San Pedro, tel. 501-226-2014, fax 226-2295; www.sanpedroholiday.com. This was one of the first hotels on the island, opening June 15, 1965.

Built and owned by Celi McCorkle, an island native and near-legend in the hospitality industry, the three-story Holiday Hotel has been well-maintained and remains a pleasant spot convenient to most everything. All rooms have A/C and some have refrigerators. Celi's Restaurant and Celi's Deli are in the hotel. Bottom Time dive shop is located on the hotel's dock. Off-season doubles are US$80 to $110, US$110-$175 in-season. Rates plus 15% tax and service charge. Bottom line: A lot like the way island hotels used to be.

★★ **Rubie's** (also known as Ruby's). Barrier Reef Drive, P.O. Box 56, San Pedro, tel. 501-226-2063, fax 226-2434; www.AmbergrisCaye.com/rubys/index.html. This is the favorite of many value-conscious visitors. Rooms in the old wooden building are basic but clean, most with shared baths; those on the street side can be a little noisy. Year-round rates: older rooms with fans and en suite baths, US$40 double (cheaper single rooms at US$20 have shared baths); rooms in a new concrete addition on the ocean side sport A/C and private baths go for around US$60 plus tax, still a good value. Good inexpensive breakfasts and light meals in the first-floor restaurant, which opens at 5 a.m. to catch the fishing crowd. The hotel is often full. Bottom line: One of the island's best values.

SOUTH EDGE OF TOWN/AIRSTRIP SOUTH:

(Listed from north to south, with those nearest town listed first.)

★★★+ **SunBreeze Beach Hotel.** Coconut Drive (P.O. Box 14), San Pedro; tel. 800-688-0191 or 501-226-2191, fax 226-2346; www.sunbreeze.net. The SunBreeze always had a great location, just steps from the San Pedro airstrip (but you won't be bothered by airport noise) and within walking distance of most of what there is to do in town. SunBreeze has been upgraded and considerably improved. Most recently a number of the rooms have been refurbished. There's a freshwater pool, above ground but nice. The pool is just steps from the excellent Blue Water Grill, where you can charge your bar and restaurant tab to your room.   Many other restaurants are within a few blocks. SunBreeze has 39 large rooms, configured in a two-story motel-style U-shape. Five of them are billed as "premier" with ameni-ties such as Jacuzzi tubs. All have strong air conditioners, tele-phones, color cable TV and tile floors. The best rooms are the deluxe rooms near the water. SunBreeze is directly on the water, with a dock and an independent dive shop, but there's a seawall and no real swimming beach. A good beach is at Ramon's nearby. The SunBreeze has handicap-accessible rooms, uncommon in Belize. Rates for doubles, in-season, US$170 to $225; off-season, US$140-$195, plus 9% tax and 6% service. Discounts for direct booking may be available. The same man-agement also operates **SunBreeze Suites** north in town, for-merly Aqua Marina Suites. Bottom line: Not luxury, but comfort-able, spacious, convenient, casual and pleasant.

★★★ + **Belizean Reef Suites.** Coconut Drive, San Pedro; tel. 330-544-4302 or 501-226-2582, fax 330-652-0026; www.belizeanreef.com. Bright white, spic 'n span one-bedroom, one-bath, two-bedroom, two-bath and three-bedroom, three-bath condos, on the sea. This is a popular spot for travelers who want a great location and lots of space. The first-floor units on the water are primo. In some units, there's air conditioning in bedrooms only. No pool, but there's a good beach close by at Ramon's. Rates (minimum four days) US$125 to $225 off-sea-son, US$160 to $245 in-season. Rates plus tax, no service charge. Lower rates for longer stays. Children under 10 not accepted. Bottom line: Very nice small condotel in a very good location.

★★★★ **The Palms.** Coconut Drive (P.O. Box 88), San Pedro; tel. 501-226-3322, fax 226-3601; www.belizepalms.com.   This three-story condotel on the water has a lot going for it: 12 attractive and well-decorated condominium apartments plus a small casita near the pool, which is small and on the back side but surrounded by tropical greenery, a sandy beach, and a con-venient location at the south edge of town. Rates off-season: one-bedroom condo, US$148-$176, two-bedroom US$200 to

$212, with discounts on week or longer stays; in-season: one-bedroom, US$204-$242, two-bedroom, US$275 to $292. Rates plus 9% hotel tax and 10% service charge. US$20 extra per person over two in the one-bedroom and four in the two-bedroom. Bottom line: Excellent option for a condo vacation.

★★★★ **Ramon's Village**. Coconut Drive, San Pedro; tel. 800-624-4415 or 601-649-1990, fax 601-649-1996; www.ramons.com.   Anyone who has heard of San Pedro has probably heard of Ramon's Village, the creation of Ambergris native and pioneering hotel operator Ramon Nuñez. Now American-owned, over the years it has grown from a small, moderately priced collection of thatched cabañas on the beach into a much larger group of multiunit buildings and individual cabañas, with 61 rooms and suites. Rates also have gone up, for some units being near the top price point on the island, but Ramon's retains its sand-and-thatch ambiance. The resort has one of the better beaches on the island. Certainly, it's the best in or near town, part of the hotel's 500-foot water frontage. A small artificial reef near the 420-foot pier brings fish to snorkelers. The pool is gorgeous, but it's smaller than it looks in the brochures. Ramon's has a room service, a popular bar, a (fairly pricey, not particularly notable) restaurant called Pineapples and a big dive operation. Rooms vary from okay to gorgeous. They are divided into three basic categories: beach front, seaside and garden view. There also are one- and two-bedroom suites with kitchenettes, including the deluxe 600 square-foot Presidential suite, and several "honeymoon cabañas." All are now air conditioned. The location, just south of the airstrip, and a five-minute stroll from town, can't be beat. Ramon's does a first-rate job of marketing, especially to travel agents, and it enjoys one of the higher occupancy rates on the island. The crowd here is usually a little younger and more active than the average at island hotels. Rates vary depending on location and date. In-season, cabañas are US$180 to $255 double and suites are US$210 to $480. Off-season rates are only a few dollars less. Rates at **Steve & Becky's,** the cottage colony annex across the street, are US$145-150 double. All rates plus 9% tax and 10% service.

Bottom line: Popular, well-located, well-run hotel that manages to retain its island ambiance despite expansion and relatively high prices.

★★★+ **Corona Del Mar.** Coconut Drive, San Pedro; tel. 501-226-2055, fax 226-2461; www.ambergriscaye.com/coronadel-mar.   This is a low profile lodging spot, also known as Woody's Wharf after the gregarious founder of the hotel, but regulars know it offers 12 pleasant rooms and four attractive apartments on the water, at moderate cost. It also has the island's first elevator, but no pool. Off-season rates US$70 to $120; in-season US$85 to $130, all plus tax and 10% service. Bottom-line: Friendly, homey place and one of the best values on the island.

★+ **Pedro's Backpackers Inn.** Seagrape Drive, San Pedro, tel. 501-226-3825; e-mail www.backpackersbelize.com.   This hostel cum budget hotel south of town isn't on the beach, but it does offer affordable accommodations – single beds with share bath start at US$10 per person. New rooms in the annex with A/C, cable and private bath go for US$50 double in-season and less in in low season. Free DSL internet, and there's a sports bar with pool table and projection TV. Also, a small swimming pool. The owner, inveterate Englishman Peter Lawrence, claims Pedro's has the best pizza in Belize. Bottom line: A place for backpackers and penny-pinchers.

★★+ **Changes in Latitudes B&B**. Coconut Drive, San Pedro, tel./fax 501-226-2986, www.AmbergrisCaye.com/latitudes/. With six small but pleasant and very clean rooms on the first level, and the helpful owners Renita and Cindy upstairs, this is a B&B with a tasty Belizean breakfast (hot entrees include breakfast tacos or Belizean eggs) served in the common room. Guests have 24-hour acess to the common and kitchen. Changes in Latitudes isn't directly on the water, but it's close. The owners have redecorated all the rooms (all have private bath, A/C and fan.) Rates US$95 double May to mid-December, US$115 rest of year, plus hotel tax (no service charge). Bottom line: Intimate little B&B within a short walk of town, but not on the seafront.

★★★ Belize Yacht Club Hotel & Marina. Coconut Drive (P.O. Box 62), San Pedro; tel. 866-589-4616 or 501-226-2777, fax 226-2768; www.islandclubresorts.com. This property has gone through several incarnations since it opened in the early 1990s, as condo colony, timeshare, temporary home to a med school and condotel. It still advertises as a timeshare, Island Club. The BYC has 40 apartment-style units built in a Mexican style. It's on the water, with a nice pool, but no real beach, as there's a sea wall. There's a bar, gift shop, gas station and marina. Also on site is a casino. Units are pleasant enough, but they're not really as deluxe as the rates. Rates for one- to three-bed-room units in-season, all with kitchens and air-conditioning, US$298 to $1,140, with the garden and pool view one-bedroom units being at the bottom of that range; off-season, US$250-$995. Be sure to ask for a discount. Bottom line: Condo-style, mixed used property on the "outskirts" of San Pedro, no beach, somewhat overpriced.

★★★ Exotic Caye Beach Resort. Coconut Drive, San Pedro; tel. 501-226-2870; www.belizeisfun.com. Formerly called Playador, this is another property that has gone through many changes over the years. Things seem to have settled down now, with the hotel offering thatch-style one- to three-bedroom units. There's a pool, a pleasant sandy beach, a dive shop and a café (open for breakfast and lunch). The bar, Crazy Canuck's, attracts a lively crowd, especially Canadians. Guests have com-plimentary use of the San Pedro Fitness Club's gym and outdoor tennis courts. The suites and rooms vary considerably in fur-nishings and amenities; in general you'll be happier in the prici-er digs. Rack rates in-season are US$165 to $345, and US$150 to $335 in summer, plus tax. Bottom line: An option in the mid-range.

★★+ Coconuts Caribbean Hotel. Coconut Drive (P.O. Box 94), San Pedro, tel. 501-226-3500, fax 226-3501, www.coconutshotel.com. Once popular with value-minded island visitors, under new management Coconuts has expanded and remodeled, adding a pool, additional rooms and restaurant. Rates have jumped to US$150 for a double room in-season, and US$215 to $360 for a suite. Room rates drop to US$100 to $205 in summer. Bottom line: We're not sure what to think.

★★★ **Coral Bay Villas.** Coconut Drive (P.O. Box 1), San Pedro; tel. 501-226-3003; www.coralbaybelize.com. One-bedroom beachfront condo suites in a white two-story concrete building with red tile roof. No pool, but there's a nice sandy beach. Offered through Southwind Realty, rates are US$120 double, off-season, US$150 in-season plus tax. Bottom-line: A pleasant small condo, but no pool.

★★★+ **Caribbean Villas.** Coconut Drive (P.O. Box 71), San Pedro, tel. 501-226-2715; www.caribbeanvillashotel.com. The folks who built and ran this place for many years, Wil and Susan Lala, sold out in 2004, and new management has added a beach bar and new swimming pool. There's a variety of accommodations in the two-level whitewashed buildings with tile roofs, from small studios to two-bedroom suites. You'll enjoy the nice beach area and pier, with a little artificial reef for snorkeling, and there are two outdoor hot tubs. There's no full-service restaurant (the beach bar serves continental breakfast and snacks) but several are nearby, as is a supermarket if you want to self-cater. A "people perch" is great for a bird's eye view of the island or for letting the birds see you. In this fast-changing island, this is one of the few hotels near town that still has a significant amount of undeveloped green space around it. Bikes are free for guests, and there are phones in rooms but no TVs. Rates are US$105-$260 double mid-December through mid-April, and only a bit less, US$95 to $210, the rest of the year. All rates plus tax (no service charge). Bottom line: Natural setting, nice beach and easy-going atmosphere make a visit here a good experience.

★★★★ **Xanadu Island Resort.** Coconut Drive, San Pedro; tel. 501-226-2814, fax 226-3409; www.xanaduresort-belize.com.

Xanadu once billed itself as the "world's first monolithic dome resort," a description which might sound good to an engineer but doesn't exactly get our poetic juices flowing. Happily, these monolithic domes look much nicer than they sound. Owner Ivan Sheinbaum one day showed us a new unit that was under construction. The building process is costly, but the result is a masonry dome with foam insulation that, according to Ivan, a Canadian originally from South Africa, is fireproof and can withstand winds of up to 300 mph. The domes are covered with thatch palapa roofs, and inside the condo suites (studios, one-, two-, and three-bedroom) are attractively furnished in earth tone colors, with central air-conditioning, fans, phones and cable TV. Free wireless internet. You get the use of bikes, canoes and kayaks gratis. There's a nice little stretch of seaside sand, though with a seawall, a 350-foot pier and a lovely freshwater swimming pool. Rates US$190 (studio) to $600 (three-bedroom) in-season and US$150 to $495 May to mid-December, plus hotel tax and 8% service charge. Bottom-line: Something different on the beach.

SOUTH END:

(This area begins about a mile south of town. Properties are listed from north to south, with those nearest town listed first.)

★★★★+ **Villas at Banyan Bay.** Coconut Drive (P.O. Box 91), San Pedro, tel. 866-352-1163 or 501-226-3739, fax 226-2766; www.banyanbay.com. At this 42-unit condotel there's all the pleasures of home … if your home happens to be just steps from the Caribbean. Many of the guests here appear to be families, and a terrific family place this is. The kids love the big, two-section pool, and dad and mom go for the fully equipped kitchen and the whirlpool off the master bedroom. The beach here, about a mile and a half south of town, is one of the best on the island, though it does have some seagrass, and there's a dive and gift shop on the pier. The food at Rico's restaurant on-site doesn't always knock us out, but service is good, and it has a beautiful setting on the water for drinks or dinner; breakfast is handy and well done. We're impressed by the space at Banyan – these units with two full baths are significantly larger than most of the other two-bedroom condo on the island. And we're impressed by the high degree of maintenance. The apartments look just as good now as when they were built several years ago. The woodwork and cabinets are mahogany. The cathedral ceilings in the main living area sport a stunning array of tropical hardwoods. There's a fitness center, too. Rates: US$275-$475 for a two-bedroom condo in-season, depending on location and number of people, and US$195-$275 in the summer. Bottom line: Upscale two-bedroom condos on the water, great for families or two couples traveling together. Villas at Banyan Bay has , been taken over and is being operated by its lender, Belize Bank.

★★★★ + **Grand Colony Villas.** Coconut Dr.; tel. 501-226-3739, fax 226/2768; www.grandcolonyvillas.com. New in 2005, the Grand Colony Villas are among the most upscale condos on the island. The 21 two-bedroom, two-bath apartments, range from 1,100 to over 1,900 square feet and have 10-foot ceilings, marble and hardwood floors, mahogany doors and cabinets, and deluxe furnishings. There is also a three-bedroom presidential suite. Rates: US$350 to $775 in season. The beach here is one of the best on the island. Bottom line: One of the most luxe properties on the island.

★★★ + **Banana Beach.** Coconut Drive (P.O. Box 94), San Pedro; tel. 501-226-3890, toll-free 877-288-1011, fax 501-226-3891; www.bananabeach.com. Under new Canadian ownership since late 2009, this resort has just about everything to make your vacation a success – a genuinely friendly staff, spacious and furnished one- to four-bedroom suites, affordable rooms and a setting just steps from the sea. The 35 original one-bedroom units are in a single three-story building, designed in a style similar to Mexican hotels, around a courtyard with swimming pool, within watermelon seed spitting distance of the sea. A three-story addition, which went up in 2002, has a variety of "expandable" suites, regular rooms and also some one-bedroom efficiencies, which are rented for longer periods (one month or longer.) The suites have fully furnished kitchens. Also added was a second pool and an air-conditioned restaurant, El Divino, featuring excellent steaks and killer martinis. We recommend you spring for one of the seafront units, especially the second and third floor deluxe units in either the original or new building, all of which have fabulous views of the water. The hotel's tour office, Monkey Business, can set you up with tours, cart rentals and diving. Rates have risen with new management but are still a good value. Off-season, rates start at US$100 double for a room or US$125 for a courtyard suite, US$165 for a seafront one-bedroom suite and top out at US$465 for a four-bedroom seafront suite. In high season, rates range for US$115 to $530. All rates include breakfast. Bottom line: Great choice for service, value and a seafront vacation.

★★★ + **Mata Rocks.** Coconut Drive (P.O. Box 47), San Pedro; tel. 888-628-2757 or 501-226-2336, fax 226-2349; www.matarocks.com. Mata Rocks is a small beachfront hotel with 11 rooms and two junior suites, just south of Banana Beach. With its stucco and wood exterior in a distinctive white, turquoise and purple paint scheme, Mata Rocks has a comfortable, relaxed feel. The thatch beach bar hops, however, and if you want to pop into town, about 1 1/2 miles away, bikes are complimentary. All units have A/C and little fridges, and the junior suites have kitchenettes. In-season doubles US$145 to $170 for rooms and US$195 to $210 for junior suites. Summer rates US$110 to $170. Rates are plus tax but include continental breakfast and roundtrip transfers from the San Pedro airstrip. Bottom line: Relax in laidback, non-cookie cutter surroundings on the beach.

★★★★★ **Victoria House.** Coconut Drive (P.O. Box 22), San Pedro; tel. 800-247-5159 or 713-344-2340, fax 713-224-3287; www.victoria-house.com.   If what you want is an upscale but casual resort vacation, Victoria House is just about perfect. About 2 miles south of town, Victoria House is a quiet hideaway on 19 acres, with a variety of accommodations ranging from comfy motel-like rooms in two buildings at the back of the resort to rooms in the main lodge to thatch casitas (recently redone) to deluxe villas and gorgeous new condos. There has been lots of remodeling and upgrading of late, including a second fabulous pool, along with a new group of condo villas at the south edge of the resort. These new condo villas are our pick for some of the most beautiful beach accommodations in Belize. The hotel's restaurant, Palmilla, remains an asset. A full meal plan is US$75 per person per day, but many guests prefer not to be locked into a meal plan and dine around the island. A freestanding lounge cabaña on the beach is ideal for sipping rum drinks or Belikins. Head to the sandy beach area for relaxing, or swim off the pier. The hotel also has a gift shop and a dive operation. Service is top-notch everywhere. Victoria House is a popular place to get married, and the hotel has honeymoon packages. Rates for rooms in-season are June through mid-December, US$180 to $312, suites US$375 to $495; villas, condos and houses, US$595 to $1775. Rates a little lower off-season, all plus tax and 10% service. Rates higher during holiday periods. Bottom line: Upscale, barefoot hideaway.

★★★- **Royal Caribbean Resort.** 1 Seagrape St.., tel. 501-226-4220; www.ambergriscaye.com/royalcaribbean/. New in late 2005, the little yellow cabins lined up in rows at Royal Caribbean remind a lot of people of army barracks, or DFC by the Sea, but, inside, the 45 cabins are fairly spacious, with tile floors, wicker furniture, and kitchenettes, and all have cable TV and air conditioning. There's a pool and 400 feet of beach immediately next door (south) of Victoria House. The prices, US$125 double off-season and US$140 in-season, are attracting some guests. (All rates plus tax.) A restaurant is on-site. Bottom line: Simplicity and value, if not style, at the south end of the island.

★★★ **Sunset Beach Resort.** Coconut Drive, San Pedro; toll-free 866-527-8851 or tel. 501-226-3504; www.condosinbelize.com. This condotel is one of the last hotels on the South End (farther south are private homes and Pelican

Reef), about a US$10 cab ride from town. There are one-, two- and three-bedroom units, and there's a nice pool. The beach has a seawall. Rates US$165 to $195 in season, double, plus US$25 per additional person. Off-season rates are slightly less. Bottom line: A quiet place for families and larger groups.

★★★ **Miramar Villas.** Coconut Drive, San Pedro; tel. 501-www.miramarvillas.net. This seafront condo development, just south of Sunset Beach, opened in late 2006. It has two build-ings, one with six two-bedroom, two-bath units of about 1400 sq. ft., and the other has four units of varying sizes. There is an infinity-edge pool, a pier, and the property is gated and fenced. The beach has a a low seawall. Rates for a seafront two-bed-room condo in-season are US$230, off-season US$200. Three-bedroom units go for US$335 in and US$290 out. Bottom line: Another nice condotel option on the South End.

★★★★ + **Pelican Reef Villas.** Coconut Dr., 501-226-2352; 281-394-3739 in the U.S.; www.pelicanreefvillas.com.
While listening to the pool's tinkling waterfall, it is easy to believe you've stumbled upon a hidden tropical treasure, when really the faux cave is a swim-up bar and Pelican Reef is only a little south of San Pedro's bustle. This condotel is one of the most popular on the island, despite relative spendy rates. Large alabaster buildings with butter-yellow trim house the 24 two-bedroom (US$436 including tax for up to four people) and three-bedroom (US$682 for up to six) units. Tastefully decorat-ed, with fully equipped kitchens, mahogany cabinets, granite countertops and plush sleigh-beds, the units are gorgeous and the oceanfront views are stunning. No restaurant on site. The same owners operate **Athens Gate,** a new 12-unit condotel nearby that can be booked through Pelican Reef.

NORTH AMBERGRIS:

These hotels are all north of the river channel. Depending on the golf cart trail condition, you can go by cart as far north as around Portofino. Most people, however, take a water taxi or the regularly scheduled Island Ferry or Coastal Xpress. Hotels are listed south to north, with those nearest town listed first.

★★★ **Reef Village.** North Ambergris, just north of the bridge, on the lagoon side; tel. 501-226-4311; www.reefvillagebelize.com. The first large complex you'll come to after crossing the bridge to North Ambergris, on the lagoon side, is this monument to unfortunate taste. Condos here start at around US$130,000, so quite a few of them have sold. If you're on a golf cart, you may be stopped by a time share tout trying to sell you a week or two. Vacation packages including lodging, three local dives and a snorkel trip are around US$1,500 for two. The same developer wants to do the giant South Beach project at the southern tip of the island. There is a new movie and a live performance theater at the resort -- it's called the **Paradise Theater.** Bottom line: Good place to see a movie.

★★★ **The Cloisters.** North Ambergris, just north of the bridge, on the sea side; tel. 501-226-2816; www.ambergriscaye.com/cloisters/index.html. A cluster of condos, with rates from US$135 to $220 in-season, and US$85 to $145 off, plus tax. Bottom: Convenient to town.

★★★ **Ak'bol Yoga Retreat & Eco-Resort**. North Ambergris; tel. 501-226-2073; www.akbol.com. This hip little resort has seven simple thatch cabañas (US$135-$150 in-season), some with sea views, around a natural stone swimming pool. You'll love the outdoor showers in the cabañas. On the lagoon side is a three-story building with 30 single rooms (shared baths) for those attending yoga retreats. Rates for these rooms start at US$35 plus tax per person, and yoga lessons are US$15. Bean, the restaurant, serves local foods such as salbutes, panades, and pupusas at some of the lowest prices on the island, and it also offers pizzas and vegetarian dishes. Shade, the bar, has cold drinks at reasonable prices. Bottom line: Cool, small laid-back resort, rooms and restaurant are bargains.

★★★★ + Grand Caribe Suites and Residences. Tres Cocos area of North Ambergris; tel. 501-226-4726; www.grandcaribe.com. Tim Jeffers' latest project on the island is a beaut! Set in an arc on a 5-acre beachfront site, Grand Caribe's 74 luxury condos, in eight four-story, red-tiled-roof clusters, face the sea and a 500-foot stretch of sandy beach. Grand Caribe debuted in 2008, with the last units opening in 2010. The one, two- and three-bedroom suites (US$365 to $695 in-season, US$275-$525 off-season, plus hotel tax) have Brazilian floor tiles, kitchens with granite countertops and mahogany cabinets and high-quality furnishings. Rare in Belize, some units have elevator access. An unusual feature is the long, curving pier with berths for a number of boats. Bottom line: New luxury condos, all with views of the sea, short bike or golf cart ride to restaurants and to town.

★★★ Cocotal Inn & Cabanas. North Ambergris, about 2.5 miles north of the center of town; tel. 501-226-2097; www.cocotalbelize.com. Looking for small, comfy spot on the beach? Cocotal could be it. There are only four units - two cottages and two suites in the main house. Our favorite is the casita - with vaulted hardwood ceiling and a four-poster queen bed. It's closest to the beach and also overlooks the pool. All have fully equipped kitchens, so you can cook your own meals, or hop on one of the complimentary bikes and ride to a nearby restaurant. The helpful owners are on-site. Rates: US$125-$250 in-season, US$100-$200 off-season, plus tax. Bottom line: Friendly, homey small resort on the beach, affordable rates.

★★★ + El Pescador. P.O. Box 17, San Pedro; tel. 501-226-2398, fax 226-2977; www.elpescador.com.   For more than a quarter century, El Pescador has been the island's leading fishing lodge. Today, it's bigger and more upmarket than it used to be, with a pool, villas and other resort amenities, but it's still devoted to anglers and angling. The focus here is on catching tarpon, bonefish, permit and jacks, but you can enjoy a fine meal, served family style in the dining room, or enjoy a drink and a Cuban cigar on the verandah. The lodge has 14 comfortable but hardly luxurious units in a rambling two-story colonial-style building with mahogany floors. Adjoining the lodge are new two- and three-bedroom villas, and these are deluxe, with prices to match. El Pescador's emphasis is on fishing packages, which include guide, boat, transfer from Belize City, meals and taxes, but there also are family and couples packages.   About the only extras are drinks, tips for guides and purchases of any fishing gear. These packages start at US$1,495 per person for three nights (two persons per room and two per boat) and range up to over US$5,020 per person for a week (one person in a room and one per boat). Bottom-line: The place on the island for serious, well-heeled anglers.

★★ + **Capricorn,** P.O. Box 247, San Pedro; tel. 501-226-2809, fax 220-5091 www.ambergriscaye.com/capricorn/index.html. Under new ownership as of late 2006, the Capricorn restaurant has regained some of its lost lustre. Capricorn the resort still has three cozy, hand-built wooden cabins, all with air condition-ing. Double rates off-season US$155, in-season US$185, includ-ing continental breakfast, plus tax and 10% service. Bottom-line: Small, cozy cabins. *(See separate review of restaurant, below.)*

★★★ **Captain Morgan's,** San Pedro; tel. in the U.S. 888-653-9090, fax 307-587-8914; www.belizevacation.com. Those thatch cabañas you saw on the first Fox TV *Temptation Island* series were filmed at Captain Morgan's. These days, you may spot more timeshare salespeople than jiggling bare flesh. Captain Morgan's is a collection of cabañas – older but with upgrades such as air conditioning – and new condo/timeshare villas of one and two bedrooms. The resort has a nice freshwa-ter pool and the beach, while not so great for swimming, is beautiful. The resort has gone through a number of changes over the years, with a variety of managers and staff, and from reports we've heard service isn't consistently top-notch. Rates: US$199 to $420 double in-season, and a more affordable US$139 to $250 off-season, plus tax and 10% service. Bottom line: Sand, seclusion and timeshare tours.

★★★★+ **Seacape Villas,** San Pedro; tel. toll-free 888-753-5164 or 501-226-2119; www.seascapebelize.com. This collection of six upscale homes on four beachfront acres, built by noted island developers Bob and Diane Campbell, opened in 2006. Each villa has around 3,000 square feet, with a sunken living room, slate floors, outdoor garden with hot tub, and unobstruct-ed views of the sea. The homes are privately owned but man-aged by the developers, and available for rent when the owners aren't in residence. Expect to pay around US$450 to $750 per day, more for larger groups, less off-season. Bottom line: Beautiful collection of luxurious villas.

★★★+ **Belizean Shores.** P.O. Box 1, San Pedro; tel. 800-319-9026 or 501-226-2355, fax 226-2931; www.belizeanshores.com. Belizean Shores is a popular condotel choice on North Ambergris (a US$7 water taxi ride to town, each way), with good rates and a lot of space in the units. The pool is a beaut, one of the best on the island, with a swim-up bar, and huge. The beach is small but fairly nice, and the sea-grass is removed from some of the swimming area, and there's a 350-foot pier. There's free use of kayaks, so you can kayak out to the reef and snorkel. Rates US$139 to $199 double mid-April through November, US$239 to $299 in-season, plus tax. A sister resort nearby, (★★★★) **Coco Beach,** is even newer and nicer, though more expensive, with rates as high as US$649 for a two-bedroom seaview suite. Bottom line: Agreeable and popular condo development.

★★★★ **Las Terrazas.** North Ambergris, 4 miles north of town; tel. 800-447-1553 or 501-226-4249; www.lasterrazasbelize.com. Las Terrazas, which opened in late 2007, is a luxury 39-unit condominium project with two- and three-bedroom suites. Rates are US$295 to $495 in-season, US$195 to $385 off-season. The condos have 9-foot ceilings, travertine tile floors, fully equipped kitchens with Brazilian gran-ite countertops, and all the amenities including cable TV and high-speed Internet. A two-level pier sweeps out into the sea. A dive shop, White Sands Cove Dive Shop, is now on-site. When completed (originally set for late 2008 but now postponed), there will be a restaurant, fitness center and two pools (one pool is currently open). Bottom line: Upscale condos on 500 feet of beachfront.

★★★★★ **Azul Resort.** North Ambergris; tel. 501/226-4012; www.azulbelize.com. This is where we'd like to stay if we had the money — US$1,000 a day double all-inclusive (lodging, all meals, drinks, taxes, transfers), slightly higher at peak times. This new resort has only two beach villas, but, man, they are nice. The two-level villas have 20-foot ceilings with beams of mylady wood. Custom kitchens feature Viking appliances, and the cabinets and most of the furniture are made of zericote wood. Each villa has a 50-inch plasma flat-screen TV, and Bose theater system. On the rooftop, you can relax in your own hot tub. The two beach houses share a beautiful pool, 400 feet of beach, and about 10 acres of prime property. **Rojo Lounge,** run by the same couple, Vivian and Jeff, is next door for drinks in a romantic beachside setting and some of the best food on the island. Bottom line: Hip, romantic and fabulous.

★★★★ **Mata Chica.** North Ambergris, tel. 501-220-5010, fax 220-5012; www.matachica.com.   When it opened in 1997, Mata Chica raised the bar on what constitutes hip, deluxe lodging on Ambergris Caye. Mata Chica's original owners designed this resort to the hilt. Each of the 12 air-conditioned cabañas and 2 two-bedroom villas, has a fruit theme - mango, watermelon, banana, and so on - a theme that begins with the exterior color and is carried through down to the tiles in the baths. It all may be a little too much for some, but others say the colors remind them of Gaugin. New owners have made some much-needed renovations. The beach here is postcard lovely, though swimming isn't much, and a new pool opened in 2005. There's a mini-spa. Mambo, the hotel's expensive restaurant (entrees up to around US$30), offers an eclectic menu, albeit emphasizing Italian dishes and seafood. Like the lodging, Mambo is seaside monument to design, with dramatic lighting and little touches like salt and pepper shakers made from seashells. It's definitely a romantic spot for dinner. Doubles US$280 to US$415 in-season and US$215 to $295 off-season, plus tax and 10% service. Two-bedroom villas are US$725 in and US$525 off, for up to four persons. A 5,000 sq. ft. "beach mansion" is US$1,045 in-season. Rates include transfers from San Pedro and continental breakfast. Package rates also available. No children under 10. Bottom line: If you want stylish, this is it.

★★★★ **Portofino.** P.O. Box 36, San Pedro; tel. 501-220-5096, fax 226-4272; www.portofinobelize.com. One of Portofino's drawing cards is that it has thatch cabañas, fairly rare on the island. The resort, which opened in 2001 on the site of another resort, the Green Parrot, has lushly landscaped grounds, a well-liked restaurant, dive shop, thatch units including beach

cabañas, tree house suites and an 800-square-foot honeymoon suite with whirlpool. There's a new swimming pool. Rates: US$280 to $420 double in high season, US$220 to $375 in low, including continental breakfast but not taxes or 10% service. The Mansion (US$900 in-season) sleeps up to 8. Bottom line: Thatch cabañas on the beach, and more.

★★★ + **Xaman Ek.** North Ambergris. Formerly Gaz Cooper's Playa Blanca, the property is now under new ownership and is operated as a spa and small hotel. There are three two-bedroom suites and two cabañas, all with sea views. Rates in high season are US$190 to $335, and US$165 to $300 in low season. Bottom line: Another small hotel option.

★★★ **Costa Maya Reef Resort.** Fax 52 329 291 7000 in Mexico, extension 1055; www.costamayareef.com. Formerly Avalon Reef Club, and before that Casa Caribe, this place seems always to tread water as a timeshare and remote resort. High-season rates are US$189 to $259 plus tax. Off-season one-bedroom suites start at US$139 double. Bottom line: Could be okay, depending on your expectations.

★★★★ **Blue Reef Island Resort.** North Ambergris; tel. 866-825-8501; www.bluereefresort.com. About 8 miles north of San Pedro Town, Blue Reef, which opened in 2005, has one- and two-bedroom condo units in six three-story buildings, each with five or six units. The condo apartments are very attractive, with granite tile floors and 10-ft. ceilings, and all have sea views. The swimming pool also overlooks the water. They should be nice, as most sell for around half a million US. Each bedroom has a king bed. Guest rooms have satellite TV, air-conditioning and CD players. There's little within walking distance, so for company you'll have to depend on the hotel's shuttle boat into town, a 20 minute ride each way. According to all reports, the resort's restaurant has good food, or you can have groceries delivered and cook in your upscale kitchen. Rates: US$299 to $459 in-season, US$249 to $359 off-season, plus 9% hotel tax. All-inclusive packages available. Bottom line: Luxe condo colony way up north.

★★★ **Tranquility Bay.** North Ambergris; tel. 888-843-2293; www.tranquilitybayresort.com. Opened in 2006, this resort about 12 miles north of San Pedro, Tranquility Bay has 11 concrete and stucco cottages, both two-bedroom and one-bedroom, plus a budget room. This is a place to really, really get away from things, including telephones and TVs. Not everyone likes the remoteness. Rates US$120 to $315 in-season, US$95 to $250 off-season, including continental breakfast. Rates plus 10% service and 9% tax. Bottom line: Like being on a remote island.

PRIVATE ISLANDS NEARBY

★★★★★ **Cayo Espanto.** tel. in U.S. 888-666-4282 or 910-323-8355; www.aprivateisland.com. Ready, willing and able to pay US$20,000 a couple for a week's pampering, not including airfare or tax? Then Cayo Espanto, a tiny private island on the back or bay side of Ambergris, about 3 miles west San Pedro, may be for you. At Cayo Espanto, the resort staff lines up, as on the old TV show *Fantasy Island* to greet you on arrival. Cayo Espanto's American owners quickly figured out that, in Belize's economy, it's not that expensive to hire a bunch of workers to keep the staff-to-guest ratio at two to one, especially given that the island has no more than 16 guests at one time. So if you like attentive service, you definitely will get it at Cayo Espanto, including your own "houseman" who cares for your every need day or night. Start with breakfast in bed and end the evening with pisco sours (all meals and most drinks, but not wine or champagne, are included in the price) on your private dock, before bundling off to your king-size bed with its luxurious Yves de Lorme sheets. Currently there are five villas, three one-bedroom and two two-bedroom. The villas are quite large – the smallest is 1,500 square feet – and all but one have small private "plunge" pools. We especially like the units with open-air design, with walls that fold out let the Caribbean in. Having said that, the villas are not as large or as deluxe as some other

113

lodging in Belize, such as the condos at Victoria House, or the houses at Seascape or Azul Resort on North Ambergris. Meals are created by Cayo Espanto's crew of award-winning chefs and brought to your villa. Think dishes like Herbed Goat Cheese Mousse Atop Tomato Speckled Polenta Cakes with Balsamic Onion Compote. The resort offers a full range of tours, dive and snorkel trips, fishing and all the rest, but most guests seem to spend most of their time at their villas ...and for the US$75 or more more per hour they're paying to stay here, who wouldn't? The rates are like the money-is-no-object rates on villa rentals on St. Barths: US$1,195 to $2,295 double in winter, and US$1,195 to $1,995 off-season per night, including meals and most drinks, plus 9% tax and 15% service. There's a minimum stay of five nights (some exceptions to this may be made). Rates are higher during the Christmas season. Transfers from the International Airport by air are extra. Is it worth it? Obviously there are people who figure it is. Bottom line: Deluxe private cabañas on a tiny private island for those for whom money is nothing.

★★★★ Caye Chapel Island Resort. tel. 501-226-8250; www.cayechapel.com. Caye Chapel is a privately owned island just south of Caye Caulker and about 12 miles from Belize City. The island resort was developed as a corporate retreat and deluxe golfing hideaway, but for some reason, perhaps weak marketing, it has never really taken off. The owner, Larry Addington, a Kentucky mining baron, having failed to sell the island in one chunk, is trying to sell off the island piece by piece, with five villas and 14 building lots up for sale now. (Sunrise Realty in San Pedro is the sales agent.) The future of the island as a tourism destination is unclear. One thing's for sure, though: The island has Belize's only 18-hole golf course, a beautiful par-72, 7,000-yard seaside course. If golf is your game, this is the best Belize has to offer, with gorgeous views of the sea and the reef, and challenges provided by the brisk pre-vailing winds and the occasional crocodile. The clubhouse, between the front and back nines, rivals anything at a country club in the States. It has tile floors, high ceilings, imported fixtures and a bar that would knock the socks off Dean Martin's ghost. The island also is outfitted with a Olympic-size swimming pool, private airstrip and tennis courts. If you just want to visit and play golf, day rates for unlimited golf 9 am to 4 pm, golf cart and club rental, are US$150 per person, not including transport to the island -- US$20 roundtrip by water taxi from San Pedro. Day visitors who don't care to play golf are charged US$50, plus transportation. Bottom line: Paradise for duffers.

PRIVATE HOME AND VILLA RENTALS
Ambergris Caye has dozens of homes and villas that are rented on a weekly basis, with some also offered nightly. Rates start at around US$700 a week and go to over US$6,000 a week.

AGENTS FOR VACATION HOME RENTALS
These agents handle a number of different units on the island:

Ambergris Vacation Rentals, San Pedro; tel. 501-226-3856; www.ambergrisvacationrentals.com.

Caye Management, Beachfront near Wet Willy's, San Pedro; tel. 501-226-3077, fax 226-2831; e-mail cayeman@btl.net; www.cayemanagement.com.   The island's oldest and largest rental management company, Caye Management also handles long-term rentals (six months or more) of fully furnished apartments and houses.

AMBERGRIS CAYE DINING

Ambergris Caye has Belize's widest selection of restaurants, ranging from inexpensive local spots and pizza joints to a couple that will have you reaching for your Platinum Amex. The emphasis is on seafood, of course, but many restaurants also serve chicken and pork, and even steak. Lobster is usually the most-expensive item on the menu (in-season mid-June to mid-February), at around US$20 to $30. Pasta and Mexican-style dishes also are popular. After all that pricey seafood, an honest plate of Belizean beans and rice will taste real good.

Vegetarians can get by okay in San Pedro, even if you don't eat seafood. Rice and beans are ubiquitous (but often these are seasoned with lard or meat). Many Mexican places do up vegetarian burritos, and of course pizza is available at many spots. Fruit plates, with mangos, pineapple, watermelon and other local fruits, are a part of breakfast at a lot of places. Many restaurants will do vegetarian versions of their specialties – just ask.

Dress on the island is very casual. Even at the spiffiest places, tee-shirt and shorts are okay, although some guests at the top restaurants will wear casual resort clothes – a light summer dress or a golf shirt with khakis.

Reservations are usually not necessary, except where noted. During the season, at popular dining spots, you may have to wait a few minutes, or longer. Grab a Belikin and relax while you wait.

Keep in mind that small restaurants on a resort island can change overnight, with the loss of a cook or a setback in the personal life of the owner. Always ask locally if the restaurant you're thinking about is still good.

Our star rating system is based on a number of factors — first and foremost the quality of the food. However, service, atmosphere, setting and value also play a role. A hole-in-the-wall take-out joint may have the world's best fried chicken, but even so it won't earn four or five stars. Our system:

★★★★★ One of finest restaurants in Central America and the Caribbean, with food, service and atmosphere of a uniquely high standard. Worth a special trip just to dine here.

★★★★ One of the top restaurants in all of Belize, with outstanding food, service and atmosphere. Go out of your way to experience it.

★★★ A superior restaurant, with excellent food and, in most cases, very nice atmosphere and good service. May also be a good value.

★★ A dependably good place to eat, with well-prepared food and above-average atmosphere and service. May also offer excellent value.

★ Recommended for unpretentious food, well-prepared, where you get your money's worth.

Price ranges shown are for typical meals for one (usually dinner), not including tip, tax or alcoholic drinks.   Price ranges:

Inexpensive: Under US$5
Moderate: US$6-$15

Expensive: US$16-30
Very Expensive: Over US$30

IN TOWN OR NEARBY:

★★★★+ **Blue Water Grill.** At SunBreeze Hotel, Coconut Drive; tel. 501-226-3347. Blue Water Grill aims high, and usually hits the spot. Try the mixed seafood grill or the local snapper dusted in cumin. The crispy Coconut Shrimp is a winner. Many dishes are Asian-influenced. One or two nights a week sushi is offered. Often jammed. Open for lunch and dinner. Expensive/Very Expensive.

★★★★ **Red Ginger.** Barrier Reef Drive, at The Phoenix; tel. 501-226-4623. With its stylishly minimalist décor, this new restaurant could be in L.A., but it's actually at The Phoenix condos at the north end of San Pedro. No sea views here - you gaze at deep red and rich cream walls, with brown earth-toned accents, and tropical wild ginger plants in glass vases. The specialty is seafood. The service is a notch above most other places in San Pedro. Expensive/Very Expensive.

★★★★ **Wild Mango's.** Barrier Reef Drive, south near the town library. Award-winning chef Amy Knox moved here from Victoria House, bringing her "New Wave Latin" cooking with her. She quickly made Wild Mango's one of the top restaurants on the island. One of the specialities is ceviche, not just one kind but a variety of different ceviches. You can try a sampler, the Three Amigos. Knox also delivers some great Mexican dishes and, of course, seafood. The snapper is particularly good. Open for lunch and dinner. Moderate/ Expensive.

★★★★ **Sunset Grill.** On the lagoon side of town, tel. 501-226-2600. Seafood is the specialty here, with the snapper dishes all very good, and after your meal you can feed the tarpon in the lagoon. Per the name, the sunset views are lovely. Open for lunch and dinner. Expensive/Very Expensive.

★★★+ **Elvi's Kitchen.** Pescador Drive, tel. 501-226-2176, fax

226-3056. Yes, it's a little touristy, and yes, the waiters are a little hyper, and, yes, it's a little more expensive than some, but Elvi's does a fine job with fish and just about everything. Doña Elvia Staines began her restaurant as a take-out burger stand in 1974. It has grown in fame and fortune year after year, until today it is probably the best-known restaurant in Belize. There are still burgers on the lunch menu (around US$6) along with shrimp and fish burger versions. At dinner, you choose from large selection of seafood, chicken and other dishes, and almost all of it is good, with prices mostly under US$15 for most entrees. We always enjoy our meals here. The sand floor and the frangipani tree around which the main dining room is built add atmosphere. Open for lunch and dinner. Moderate to Expensive.

★★★ **El Fogon.** 2 Triggerfish St., just north of airstrip; tel. 501-206-2121. This locally owned restaurant serves Creole and Mestizo food cooked on a traditional hearth fire or *fogon*. The atmosphere is also traditional, with its bench seats and thatch. Currently open for lunch only. Monday-Saturday. Moderate.

★★★ **JamBel Jerk Pit.** Barrier Reef Drive, at the Coral Beach Hotel (there's also a location in Belize City). Take a fat Belizean grouper and jerk it Jamaica style and whattyagot? Some of the spiciest, tastiest food in San Pedro, that's what. The chicken wings, jerk-style pork, fish and chicken are all delicious. Open for lunch and dinner. Moderate.

★★★ **Cocina Caramba.** Pescador Drive; tel. 501-603-1652. Owner Rene Reyes has made a big success out of Caramba by simply serving good food in large portions at moderate prices. This spot is usually packed. Just about any of the seafood and Mexican dishes are tasty and well-prepared. Open for lunch and dinner. Moderate.

★★★ **Caliente.** Spindrift Hotel, Barrier Reef Drive. This restaurant, run by Jenny Staines and her partner, gets attention for its spicy versions of traditional favorites such as conch ceviche, its big variety of seafood and Mexican dishes and for its delicious soups. Locally popular for lunch, and open for dinner, too. Moderate/Expensive.

★★★ **Estel's-by-the-Sea.** Barrier Reef Drive, tel. 501-226-2019. Charlie and Estella Worthington run this little seaside restaurant near Central Park. With its sand floor and piano (you ain't heard piano until you hear it played on a sand floor), this place reeks with atmosphere. It's a favorite spot for breakfast, with all the usual egg-and-bacon basics including fried potatoes, but you'll also enjoy the burritos and huevos rancheros. Opens early, closed Tuesdays. Free Wi-Fi, too. Moderate.

★★ **The Reef.** Pescador Drive, tel. 501-226-3212. This local favorite serves tasty Belizean fare such as stew chicken with rice and beans in large portions at small prices. Open for lunch and dinner. At lunch, there's a daily special for a few dollahs. Inexpensive to Moderate.

★★ **Fido's.** Barrier Reef Drive, tel. 501-226-3714. (Pronounced FEE-doh's.) Extremely popular, centrally located spot for a beer and a bite. Sit under the big palapa by the sea and enjoy burgers, fish and chips or lobster burrito. Live music many nights. Moderate.

★★ **Celi's Restaurant.** San Pedro Holiday Hotel, Barrier Reef Drive, tel. 501-226-2014. Celi's, on the beach side of the Holiday Hotel, is one of the long-established, unpretentious eateries on the island. Fish is a specialty, and it won't cost you an arm and a leg. You can dine inside or in a screened area by the beach. Open for lunch and dinner. Moderate/Expensive. **Celi's Deli** (★+, Inexpensive), for quick snacks, sandwiches, and meat pies, is nearby.

★★ **BC's Beach Bar.** Tel. 501-226-3289. Named after the owners, Bruce and Charlene, BC's is on the beach just south of SunBreeze. Don't miss the Sunday afternoon barbecue here. On Tuesday evenings, they do burgers on the beach. Other times, it's popular with the drinking crowd. Moderate.

★+ **DandE's Frozen Custard.** Pescador Dr. next to Cocina Caramba; tel. 501-608-9100. Dan and Eileen (DandE, get it?) Jamison, who used to run the local weekly paper, the San Pedro Sun, now operate this custard and sorbet shop. For something with an island flavor, try the mango sorbet or the soursop frozen custard. Inexpensive.

★+ **Rubie's** (or Ruby's), Barrier Reef Drive, tel. 501-226-2063. If you can't sleep or are heading out for a day of fishing, get up early and grab a casual breakfast at Ruby's. For a few dollars, you can enjoy coffee, burritos and the best coconut tarts on the island. Later in the day, there are sandwiches and daily specials. It starts serving around 5 a.m., and usually stays open until just after lunch. Inexpensive.

★+ **Casa Pan Dulce Bakery.** Boca del Rio area north, with a second location at the corner of Pescador Drive and Buccaneer; tel. 501-226-3242. Formerly La Popular, Pan Dulce has the best baked stuff on the island. It has a huge selection of more than 70 kinds of breads and pastries, all baked fresh locally. Inexpensive.

★ **Street vendors** offer food that is cheap, good and safe to eat. Most are in stalls at Central Park. You can get a whole plate full of delicious food for a few bucks. Don't worry – it won't upset your tummy. Also don't miss the **Lions Club** barbecue on Friday and Saturday nights. The barbecue is great and the flan is out of this world. The money also goes to a good cause – improved health care on the island. Inexpensive.

SOUTH OF TOWN

★★★★ **Hidden Treasure.** Escalante area, tel. 501-226Hidden away on a back street in a residential neighborhood south of town, Hidden Treasure won Belize Restaurant of the Year from the Belize Tourism Board in 2009. At dinner, you dine by candlelight, in the sultry tropical air under a pitched roof set off by bamboo, mahogany and cabbage bark wood. The signature BBQ ribs are seasoned with traditional Garifuna spices and glazed with pineapple or papaya sauce. Mojarro a la Lamanai (US$20) is snapper seasoned with Mayan spices and cooked in a banana leaf. Expensive/Very Expensive. Surprisingly, it's for sale.

★★★+ **Victoria House Restaurant.** Coconut Drive at Victoria House resort, tel. 501-226-2067. The main restaurant at Victoria House, Palmilla, once dependent on unexciting buffets, has had a marked change for the better under a succession of innovative chefs. For dinner, dine by romantic candlelight. Breakfast by the pool is memorable. Expensive to Very Expensive.

★★★+ **Pinocchio Italian Restaurant & Pizzeria.** Seagrape Dr., tel 501-226-4447. New in 2009, this trattoria imports rarities to San Pedro like gorgonzola cheese and Italian salami and provides a true taste of Italy. Covered seating that is open to the air gives an island ambience, while the brick pizza oven, fresh pasta and the staff's authentic accents are reminders that the owners hail from Rome. Expensive.

★★★ **El Divino.** Coconut Drive at Banana Beach; tel. 501-226-3890. This air-conditioned restaurant (there's also seating outside) has some of the best steaks around. Also try the wood-fired pizza. The bar serves big, ice-cold martinis. Expensive.

★★+ **Rico's Bar & Grill.** Coconut Drive, at Villas at Banyan Bay. Food is only so-so, but no other restaurant on the island has a better seaside setting than Rico's. It's right on the beach. This is a fine place for breakfast or lunch on the water. After your lunch, you can feed your leftovers to the "pet" moray eels that hang out at waterside. Dinners are on the pricey side, but, again, the seaside setting is wonderful. Moderate/Expensive.

★★ **George's Kitchen.** Coconut Drive, across from Woody's Wharf. This casual spot has good breakfasts, and for value and simple good eating, you'll like it for other meals, too. Moderate.

★+ **Ali Baba.** Coconut Drive, on the east side near the airstrip. Excellent, high-value takeout roast chicken (whole chicken, US$8) and Middle Eastern dishes like hummus. Inexpensive to Moderate.

★+ **Antojitos San Telmo.** Coconut Drive near Villas at Banyan Bay, tel. 501-226-2921. It's just a joint, but a good joint, with snacks like tacos and burritos for almost nothing. Inexpensive.

★+ **Tropical Takeout.** Coconut Drive near airstrip.. Good local lunches at modest prices -- like four delicious chicken tacos for US$2.50. Inexpensive/Moderate.

NORTH AMBERGRIS

★★★★★ **Rojo Lounge and Market.** At Azul Resort; tel. 501-226-4012. This may be is the hippest restaurant in Belize. It enjoys a romantic beachside setting, where you can watch the Caribbean change colors by day or the stars flicker at night. There's even a pool, if you feel like taking a dip. Try the conch pizza or grouper stuffed with cashew-crusted lobster. The guava-glazed ribs are a specialty. Killer mojitos, too. Rojo Market has groceries and prepared foods for takeout. You'll want to take a water taxi here. Expensive to Very Expensive.

★★★★ **Rendezvous.** Next door to Journey's End, tel. 501-226-3426. We'll meet you here! This may be the first Thai-French fusion restaurant in Central America and surely it's the best. Run by expats who formerly lived in Southeast Asia and else-where, with expert help from local cooks, Rendezvous has become one of the top restaurants on the island. With just 24 seats, the setting is intimate, on the second floor of a colonial-style house by the water. The menu changes frequently, but you can expect dishes such as pad thai or chicken in a red curry coconut sauce. The restaurant even makes its own wines (from imported grape juice). Reservations for dinner suggested. Reached by water taxi. Expensive to Very Expensive.

★★★★ **Capricorn**. About 3 miles north of San Pedro, tel. 501-

123

226-2809. After a brief downturn in quality, under new owners Capricorn has regained its sea legs and once again is one of the best restaurants on the island. If there's a weakness, it is that the chef stays with proven winners, such as filet mignon and grilled lobster (each US$38, plus tax and service) and rarely opts for innovation. The seaside setting is romantic. Reservations essential. Get here by water taxi. Very Expensive.

★★★ + **Mambo.** Mata Chica Beach Resort; tel. 501-220-5010. Wow! If you'd visited the island a few years ago, you'd never have thought Ambergris Caye would get this kind of place. The restaurant space is open, appealing and upscale. Everything is designed to the hilt – even the menus show hours of design time. On those menus is a selection of sophisticated Italian dishes and seafood, along with daily specials. But you need to bring plenty of money or plastic. Open for lunch and dinner. Reached by water taxi. Very Expensive.

★★★ + **Aji Tapa Bar and Restaurant.** Beachfront, Buena Vista area, North Ambergris (about 2 1/2 miles north of town centre), tel. 501-226-4047. Relax in a shady seaside patio, with views of the beach and barrier reef in the distance, and snack on delicious small plates of barbecue shrimp, bacon-wrapped dates, and a heavenly artichoke dip. For a special treat, try the seafood paella. Expensive.

★★★ + **Legends Burger House.** Tres Cocos area, North Ambergris, on the golf cart path at the site of the former Sweet Basil, tel. 501-226-2113. Burgers and nothing but burgers, but they are excellent at this "American-style burger joint." New in late 2009, Legends already has a big following. Burgers, which come with crisp fries, are reasonably priced, from around US$6 to $10. Chili fries are US$6, and an ice-cold draft Belikin is US$2.50. Moderate.

★★★ + **Lazy Croc BBQ.** Just north of Grand Caribe, about 2 1/2 miles north of town centre, tel. 501-226-4015. As befits a BBQ joint, the menu here is short and sweet - pulled pork, BBQ chicken, ribs, Buffalo wings and chili, with sides of coleslaw, French fries, BBQ beans and macaroni and cheese. Barbecue platters with garlic toast and two sides are US$8-$15. Lazy Croc is only open only three days a week (11-6 Friday-Sunday). And, yes, there are real crocs in the lagoon near the restaurant, but don't give them leftovers. Moderate/Expensive.

WHERE TO PARTY

For visitors, San Pedro is the nightlife capital of Belize. Still, San Pedro is not exactly a world-class party town. Nightlife usually consists of drinks and dinner at a local restaurant, with perhaps a later visit to one of the "clubs" or hotel beach bars, a few of which rev up late and don't stop until 4 or 5 a.m. Quite a few expats on the island have made a career out of drinking.

Big Daddy's is probably the hottest spot on the island, and things sometimes go late and loud here. Across the street, **Jaguar's** hops, too, especially toward the weekend. The real action at these spots often doesn't get started until midnight. **Fido's** is always busy, with lots of people dropping in for a drink or to hear some music. **BC's, Wet Willy's** and the **Tackle Box** are popular bars where you can get a cold beer or something stronger. **Pedro's** is a local expat hangout, and some days there's a poker game going in the back room. **Cholo's** and a couple of other small bars have pool tables. Several hotels have popular beach-side bars, including the **Pier Lounge** at the Spindrift Hotel, (home of the chicken drop), Ramon's **Purple Parrot,** Exotic Caye's **Crazy Canucks, Coconut's** bar, Mata Rocks' **Squirrel's Nest** beach bar. You can stroll along the beach south of town and slake your thirst at a half dozen beach bars.

A long-time small casino on the island, the Palace Casino – where the slogan was "It Ain't Vegas" – has closed. A larger casino is open at the **Belize Yacht Club,** but it still ain't Vegas. For more action, you can try the **Princess Casino** in Belize City. There also are three sizeable casinos in the Commercial Free Zone near Corozal Town (a 25-minute flight away).

DAY TRIPS AND TOURS

You can use San Pedro as a base to tour much of Belize, including other cayes and much of the mainland. You can even do a day trip to Tikal. Most hotels will help you arrange tours and guides. Prices, schedules and destinations change regularly, depending on the weather, the season, the particular guide and how many other people want to go, so it's best to wait until you get on the island to make your tour plans.

If you are independent-minded, you can put together your own day trips and perhaps save money. For example, instead of paying US$125 or more per person for a day tour of the Belize Zoo and points west, find another couple to share the costs, grab a map and guidebook, take the ferry to Belize City (or fly into municipal airport) and rent a car for the day. On a day trip, you can easily visit the Belize Zoo, Xunantunich and Cahal Pech ruins and see something of San Ignacio. Done this way, your cost should be less than US$50 or $60 per person including your share of car rental, gas and entrance fees.

However, a guide can add a lot to the quality of your sightseeing. All guides in Belize—there are about 1,200 — must attend training and are licensed by the government. The **San Pedro Tourist Guide Association** is in the Town Hall on Barrier Reef Drive, tel. 501-226-2391.

Some tours include soft drinks, beer or rum punch and lunch in the tour price. Children 12 and under are usually charged at one-half to three-fourths of the adult rate shown below.

Here's information on few of the popular day trip and tour options, with price ranges:

★★★ **Belize Zoo/Western Belize:** This trip usually begins with a flight on Maya Island or Tropic to the municipal airport, where you connect with a shuttle bus which takes you on the Western Highway for a visit to the wonderful Belize Zoo, maybe a quick peep at Belmopan, Belize's mini-capital, lunch and perhaps a tour of Xunantunich, a Classic Period Maya site. Some trips also include a visit to the Mountain Pine Ridge, including stops at Thousand Foot Falls and Rio Frio cave. Around US$125 per person.

★★★★ **Lamanai Ruins:** Most of these trips start with a short boat ride across the lee waters of Ambergris to the mainland, then short van ride, and then a boat trip up the beautiful New River. You will see many birds and perhaps manatees, crocodiles and other wildlife. Lamanai has a wonderful setting on the New River Lagoon. You'll get a private tour of this Maya site and likely will see a troop of black howler monkeys. Tours often includes lunch at Lamanai Outpost Lodge. This is a long, full-day and sometimes a tiring tour, but it's one of our favorites. We especially recommend **Tanisha Tours** (tel. 501-226-2314) for this trip. About US$110-$125 per person.

★★ **Altun Ha Ruins:** You go by boat across to the mangrove cut, where you transfer to a van to visit this Maya site, which dates back some 2,000 years, on the Old Northern Highway. Not as spectacular a trip as Lamanai. May include lunch at Maruba Spa. About US$75-$90 per person.

★★★ **Cave Tubing:** This is definitely one of the most exciting and interesting of all the tours you can take. Typically, you fly to Belize City, then take a van to Jaguar Paw Lodge near

Belmopan or, on some tours, to Ian Anderson's Cave's Branch Jungle Camp off the Hummingbird Highway. You hike a mile or two through broadleaf jungle and then float, on oversized inner tubes, slowly down the river. At some points, you tube through caves, some of which have Maya artifacts such as pottery. After heavy rains in the summer, the water levels may be too high to go through the caves. Some tours combine cave tubing with a visit to the Belize Zoo. Prices vary, but expect to pay about US$120 to $150 per person. If you want a zip line tour as well, figure about US$175 plus tax. If you have your own transportation, you can also go on your own for a fraction of that cost. You park in a parking lot near the Caves Branch River and Jaguar Paw Lodge, rent an inner tube and pay a small fee. Total cost, around US$15-$20 plus transportation costs.

★★ **Baboon Sanctuary:** You go by boat to the mainland, then up the Belize River to the Community Baboon Sanctuary area. Trips to the Baboon Sanctuary sometimes are combined with trips to the Belize Zoo or Altun Ha. About US$75 per person. Combination trips are around US$100-$110.

★★ **Bacalar Chico:** Bacalar Chico National Park and Marine Reserve is about 20 miles north of San Pedro and can be reached only by boat. Most tours focus on snorkeling, with several stops along the way and several in the park. You usually also stop at the park visitor center and walk around a bit. Around US$90 to $100.

★★ **Crooked Tree Wildlife Sanctuary:** Birders will want to investigate this trip. It usually includes a round trip flight to the municipal airport in Belize City where tour members are met by a van and driven up the Northern Highway to Crooked Tree, one of the main birding centers in the country. Around US$100 to $125 per person.

★★★★ **Caye Caulker:** A day trip to Ambergris Caye's "little sister" island can be done by water taxi or day sail. If the latter, the trip is usually packaged with a snorkeling tour, with stops at several small islands. Several catamarans do this trip. US$50 to $75 per person. Water taxi *(see Caye Caulker MiniGuide below)* is US$7.50 one-way.

★★★★★ **Actun Tunichil Muknal:** It is difficult to arrange a tour of this amazing cave from San Pedro, since it is a full-day tour, but if you can do so it's well worth the effort. You will probably have to stay overnight in Belmopan or San Ignacio. You'll see Mayan artifacts and skeletons. For many people, this is the highlight of their sightseeing in Belize. Only a few tour operators, all in Cayo, currently are authorized to do this trip. You'll pay around US$90 plus transport from San Pedro.

★★★ **Manatee Watching:** Belize is home to a large population of West Indian manatees. You can see these gentle mammals at the mouth of the Belize River, around Gales Point and else-where. There are strict regulations about boats approaching manatees, and visitors are not supposed to be in the water with them. Manatee watching trips are often combined with snorkel trips. US$90 per person.

★★★★★ **Tikal:** The Tikal ruins in the Petén district of Guatemala are, in excavated area at least, larger and more spectacular than any Maya site in Belize. It's an astounding place. The only way to get there and back in one day from San Pedro is to fly to the air strip at Flores/Santa Elena, Guatemala. Several tour companies and Tropic Air offer day trips from San Pedro, around US$250 to $300 per person, plus exit taxes for Belize and Guatemala.

TOUR OPERATORS
Among the many tour outfits offering trips are the following. Note that most of the dive shops listed in the Dive section above can also arrange fishing and snorkeling trips.

Belize Trips: Katie Valk, an ex-New Yorker, has lived in Belize for years and knows the country backwards and forwards.

Though she is based in Belize City and Placencia, she can arrange almost any tour or trip. She also can make hotel reservations for you in other parts of the country, and it's nice to have someone in the country to help if anything goes wrong. Tel. 501-223-0376, 501-610-1923 or 561-210-7015 in the U.S.; e-mail info@belize-trips.com, www.belize-trips.com. Although she is not in Belize, another knowledgeable travel agent who can help you arrange hotels and tours is **Barbara Kasak** of **Barb's Belize.** Tel. 888-321-2272 or 315-673-2202; email escape@BarbsBelize.com, www.barbsbelize.com.

Elbert Greer, Guide: Elbert Greer is one of Belize's top bird experts. He also authored a book on birding in Belize, called *Birdwatching with Bubba.* Needless to say, his birding tours are excellent, and he also does dive, fishing and Maya trips. Based at Las Terrazas, Greer offers scuba lessons and runs dive trips. Tel. 501-226-3528. http://scubalessonsbelize.blogspot.com/

Captain "'Lil Alfonse" Alfonso Graniel: Excellent snorkel and fishing trips, and other boat trips. Tel. 501-226-3537; e-mail alfonso@ambergriscaye.com, www.ambergriscaye.com/alfonso/index.html.

Excaliber Tours: An experienced dive and tour operator, with about half a dozen boats and a full stable of dive trips and tours. Tel. 501-226-3235; www.ambergriscaye.com/excalibur/index.html.

Monkey Business Travel Shoppe: Located at Banana Beach, Monkey Business doesn't run any tours itself, but it can book just about any trip or tour you want, plus mainland hotel reservations, golf cart rentals, and other activities. Tel. 501-226-3890; email tours@bananabeach.com, www.ambergristours.com.

SEAduced by Belize/SEA Belize: Local, family-run operation offers a range of tours, from manatee watching at Goff's Caye to Lamanai and Altun Ha Maya tours. Also available are kayaking trips on the lagoon side of Ambergris. Tel. 501-226-3221; www.seaducedbybelize.com.

SEArious Adventures: SEArious offers mainland and water trips. Tel. 501-226-2690; www.ambergriscaye.com/searious/index.html.

Tanisha Tours: A class operation, and one of the best tour outfits in Belize, Tanisha pioneered the Lamanai tour from San Pedro and also does manatee watching tours and trips to Altun Ha and elsewhere. Tel. 501-226-2314; www.tanishatours.com.

WATERSPORTS

Powerboat rentals: You likely will find it impossible to rent a small powerboat to go fishing or snorkeling on your own. The shallow, tricky waters inside the reef and the danger of hitting a coral head makes San Pedranos reluctant to rent their boats to someone who isn't familiar with local waters. However, you can charter a small power boat with captain for around US$250 a day to take you and your party of around two to four people to visit other nearby cayes. Most hotels and dive shops will be able to arrange the charter for you – try to give at least one day's advance notice.

Small sailboat rentals: Small sailboats, both monohull and catamaran, are available for rent. Expect to pay around US$20 to $50 an hour. Sailing lessons run around US$50 an hour. Contact **Sailsports Belize** at Caribbean Villas hotel (tel. 501-226-4488; www.sailsportsbelize.com.)

Kayaking: A number of hotels, including **El Pescador, Belizean Shores** and **Xanadu,** offer kayaks free to guests. Tour operator **SEAduced by Belize** (tel. 501-226-3221; e-mail seabelize@btl.net) runs kayak trips on the island's lagoon side. **Sailsports Belize** rents them for around US$10 an hour. **Blue**

Tang Inn rents kayaks with see-through bottoms.

Windsurfing: Ambergris Caye's brisk prevailing winds and flat water inside the reef make for excellent windsurfing. The best months for windsurfing are December through July, when on average the wind is 11 to 16 knots for at least two hours for 60% of the days; from January through April it's 80% of the days. Some resorts offer windsurfing equipment to guests at no charge, or rent boards. For some of the best equipment, including more than 20 windsurfing boards in various styles and sizes, check with **Sailsports Belize,** (tel. 501-226-4488; e-mail www.sailsportsbelize.com.) Rental rates start at US$22 an hour, US$49 for a full day and US$247 a week. Sailsports Belize also offers instruction for windsurfing, kitesurfing and sailing.

Parasailing: If you're brave enough you can parasail above the reef, watching sharks and rays gliding in the water below

you. Most of the time you won't even get your feet wet, as the operator gently guides you back to the boat. However, if the wind is strong, you could be in for a rip-roaring ride. In general, it's said not to be a good idea to go parasailing when the wind is over 16 or 17 knots, which can frequently be the case off Ambergris, especially in the spring. Parasail operators come and go. Currently you can arrange it at Fido's in town. Rates are usually around US$70 for a solo parasail.

Ultralights: Toucan Fly, owned by former internet entrepreneur John McAfee, has five ultralight aircraft. You can soar over the island with a pilot/instructor.

SAILBOAT CHARTERS

Belize is not – and never will be – a big chartering center as, for example, is the British Virgin Islands. For one thing, stiff winds, strong currents and the barrier reef with its hidden coral heads can make navigation dicey, even for sailors who know local waters. Still, a few bareboat and crewed charters are available in Belize.

The only "name" chartering outfit with an office in San Pedro is **Tortola Marine Management (TMM)**. The Moorings has a base in Placencia, and TMM-Belize also has a branch there. TMM-Belize has a small fleet of catamarans, including sail and new motorized cats, ranging from 36 to 46 feet for bareboat and skippered chartering. Rates vary depending on the boat and time of year, but range from around US$3,000 to US$9,000 a week, not including provisions, fuel for motorized craft, or a US$20 per-person sailing fee. A skipper is an additional US$135 per day, and you'll be charged US$110 a day for a cook. Contact TMM (Belize) Ltd., Coconut Drive, San Pedro, tel. 800-633-0155 or 501-226-3026, fax 226-3072, www.sailtmm.com.

Other boats are available for cruises or captained charters:

Katkandu, San Pedro, tel. 501-226-3168,

www.ambergriscaye.com/katkandu/ , a 42-foot catamaran, makes seven-day trips to southern Belize and ten-day cruises to the Rio Dulce in Guatemala, among other sails. Prices vary depending on length of cruise and number of people. A six-night cruise for four people is around US$5,500.

El Gato, San Pedro, tel. 501-226-2264, www.ambergriscaye.com/elgato, has day cruises to Caye Caulker, with stops for snorkeling, for around US$50. Nice crews. Four-person minimum.

Winnie Estelle, San Pedro, tel. 501-226-2394, www.amber-griscaye.com/winnieestelle/ is a classic. The 66-foot Chesapeake Bay trawler was built in 1920 and lovingly restored during the 1980s. The *Winnie Estelle* is one of the largest charter boats operating in Belize, able to carry up to 40 passengers. She makes charter day trips to Caye Caulker and to snorkeling areas in the northern cayes (US$660 for up to 12 people, additional persons US$55 per person). Longer trips also are available.

GUIDE TO CAYE CAULKER

Caye Caulker is Ambergris Caye's "little sister" island – smaller, less developed and a cheaper date. Caulker, whose name derives from the Spanish word for coco plum, *hicaco,* has the kind of laidback, sandy-street, tropical-color, low-key Caribbean charm that travelers pay thousands to experience, but here they can have it for peanuts. Less than 10 miles, and about 30 minutes by boat, from San Pedro, Caye Caulker is definitely worth a day visit, and some people may decide they like Caulker as well, or better, than San Pedro.

We are often asked to compare the two islands. Here are some of the key comparisons:

• Caye Caulker is physically much smaller, under 5 miles long and half a mile wide at its widest point, roughly one-tenth the size of Ambergris Caye. Hurricane Hattie in 1961 divided the island in two parts. North of "the Split" it is mostly uninhabited mangrove, and this area is protected as a nature reserve. As on many islands, there are basically just three streets running down the island, Front, Middle and Back streets being the main ones, though there are few street signs and locals usually give directions just by saying "go down to yellow house and turn right." Most of the 300 or so listings in the Caye Caulker section of the Belize telephone directory don't even include a street name or address, just the person's name and phone number.

• Nearly all of the population of 1,400 live in the village on the south end of the island. Caye Caulker has streets of hard-packed sand and far fewer cars than San Pedro. Almost every-body gets around on foot. As on Ambergris, a majority of local residents are Mestizos who originally came to the island from Mexico, and who until recently made their living by fishing, but the island also has Creoles, some of whom consider themselves Rastafarians, gringos and others.

• While it is gradually going more upmarket, Caye Caulker remains a budget island. In the 1960s and 1970s, the island was on the "backpacker trail," a cheap place for longhaired visi-tors to relax, and smoke a little weed or sip a beer. Today, the most expensive hotel on Caulker goes for around US$160 a night, and most of the 40 or so hotels charge under US$75 dou-ble, with some as low as US$12. Most older hotels, like the houses are on the island, are wooden clapboard, often painted in tropical colors, but more recently constructed hotels are of reinforced concrete. Rooms are usually small, often with a fan and simple furnishings and foam-mattress beds. Only a few of the hotels on the island have swimming pools. Newer ones offer cable TV and air-conditioning. The official view of the island, though, emphasizes Caulker's new emphasis on middle-class tourism. Mo Miller, chair of the Caye Caulker Village Council marketing committee, says "Although Caye Caulker had been known for a backpacker's paradise, it is now an up and coming upscale charming island with a fishing village ambiance. Except for the Euro tourists in August, the island usually accommodates middle-class tourists."

• Caye Caulker has much the same mix of tourist-oriented businesses as San Pedro, but in most cases there are fewer of everything. The island has perhaps 20 simple restaurants, if you include those that operate out of somebody's back window, a few casual bars, a handful of dive shops and tour guides, sev-eral pint-sized groceries, a few gift shops, two banks and sever-al cybercafes.

• Beaches? Caulker has much less beachfront, and what beaches it has don't compare with some of the better stretches of beach on Ambergris Caye. A beach reclamation project did widen and improve the beach along the east side of the village (storms since have taken away and then given back sand). Swimming in the shallow water close to shore is mainly from piers and at "the Split."

• The pipe water, or tap water, on Caulker is not as good as on Ambergris Caye, where it mostly comes from a treated municipal system. On Caulker, it often has a sulphur smell and comes from shallow wells that may be close to septic systems. We recommend you not drink it; use bottled water or rainwater instead. A reverse osmosis water system is under construction and should be operation in 2010. Caye Caulker also has sandflies. Especially on calm days, they can be a real nuisance.

CHECKLIST TO COMPARE AMBERGRIS CAYE AND CAYE CAULKER

AMBERGRIS CAYE (often referred to as San Pedro):
* The biggest island in Belize (originally a peninsula jutting down from the Yucatan) — northern Belize
* Settled by Mestizos from Mexico
* Most popular destination in Belize (for many good reasons)
* Tends to attract a crowd in their 30s and older, mostly couples
* Some 20,000 people on the island
* # 1 area in Belize for foreign investment and expat living — second homes, condos, retirement
* Some sand streets though some of the streets are now paved with concrete cobblestones, formerly no building over three stories, but some new developments have four stories
* Significant new development taking place south of town and also on North Ambergris -- some 500 condo units recently built or are under construction on North Ambergris; large-scale development proposed for south end of island
* By far Belize's widest selection of restaurants and hotels
* Among the best top-end hotels: Victoria House, Azul Resort, Pelican Reef and Mata Chica
* Among the best condotels: Grand Caribe, Villas at Banyan

Bay, Grand Colony, The Palms, Xanadu, The Phoenix, Las Terrazas, Coco Beach
* Among the best mid-range lodging: Mayan Princess, Corona del Mar, Banana Beach, The Tides
* Among the best budget lodging: Ruby's, Sanpedrano, Pedro's Backpacker Inn
* Some shops, sizeable groceries, lots of bars and places to hear live music
* Some excellent restaurants including:
Very Expensive: Rojo Lounge, Capricorn, Red Ginger
Expensive: Blue Water Grill, Rendezvous, Elvi's, Pinnochio's, Hidden Treasure, Sunset Grill, Wild Mangos
Moderate: Caramba, Caliente
* Very nice beaches though like all beaches inside the reef somewhat narrow and with some goop bottoms and a good deal of seagrass – garbage on the beach in areas not policed by hotels
* Beaches along most of the Caribbean side (20+ miles)
* Reef just a few hundred yards offshore, closest at the far north
* Your first decision is to decide where to stay — in town, south of town, on North Ambergris near the river channel or on more remote parts of North Ambergris
* Lots of snorkel tours and day trips to the mainland to visit ruins
* Good recreational diving locally and excellent diving on day trips to Turneffe or Lighthouse atolls
* Get there by flights from international (US$63) or municipal airstrip (US$35) or by water taxi (US$10)
* Friendly and safe though usual cautions are in order — burglaries and thefts are fairly common, murders not unknown
* Transportation on the island — bikes, rental golf carts, cabs, water taxis
* Traffic in town is starting to get really bad
* New bridge over Boca del Rio (carts, bikes and pedestrians only) is helping open up North Ambergris, but cart path there is still very rough in places
* Hotels from US$15 to $500+ a night
* Small condos and vacation rental houses available US$100 to $500+ a night
* Golf available on nearby Caye Chapel (but expensive — US$150 a day)

* Tennis available at sports club and at several hotels
* Water — safe to drink from municipal system or RO/wells
* Good fishing — tarpon, bonefish and other
* Little snorkeling from shore -- best snorkeling requires a short boat ride to Hol Chan Marine Reserve including Shark-Ray Alley
* About the same amount of rain as Atlanta, Ga.

CAYE CAULKER:

* Still a charming, laidback small village atmosphere with a Caribbean resort vibe
* The main part of the island really is just one village of about 1,400 people, and on the average day maybe 300 or 400 tourists
* The vibes are laidback, easy-going, calm
* This is Ambergris Caye's little sister -- smaller and a cheaper date
* Moving more upmarket, with several condos recently opened, but it is still mostly a budget and backpacker island -- only five hotels on the island have a pool, for example
* Sand streets, few cars, you get around by shank's mare, bike or maybe a golf cart
* A mix of people on the island, Mestizos, some Creoles, a few gringos
* About 55 hotels and vacation rentals, mostly very small, with a total of around 900 rooms
* Beaches are not the island's strong point -- a little swimming from piers and one or two places south, but the Split is the main area where folks swim
* No municipal water or sewage system -- pipe water in many places smells strongly of sulphur (municipal RO water system coming)
* Best hotel on the island costs only about US$160 a night
* Iguana Reef Inn, Seaside Cabanas and CayeReef Condos are among the most "upscale" choices for Caulker, and all have pools
* Other good low-moderate choices -- Tree Tops, Trends Beachfront, Shirley's, Anchorage, Jaguar Morning Star, Lazy Iguana B&B, Caye Caulker Condos, De Real Macaw, Barefoot Beach, Maxhapan and others
* Good restaurants at the "top end" include Habaneros and Don Corleone's and good food, too, at Rosa's, Rainbow Grill, Sand Box, Syd's, Wish-Willie's, Amor y Café, Femi's, Jolly Roger and

others

* Two or three dive shops do dive trips -- snorkeling and diving here are a little cheaper than San Pedro and Placencia
• The reef is just a few hundred feet offshore
* For booze and what action there is, hit the Lazy Lizard and I&I and a few other bars
* Rastas occasionally bug you
* No golf or tennis (golf available on Caye Chapel)
* Several high-profile crimes occurred recently on island – police force has been revamped
* Getting there is easy -- it's a US$7.50 water taxi ride from Belize City or San Pedro; also, by air on Maya Island or Tropic Air, US$63 from international, US$35 from municipal

GETTING TO CAULKER

You can fly to Caulker's little airstrip on **Tropic Air** (www.tropicair.com) or **Maya Island Air** (www.mayaregional.com) from Belize City. Flights from either International or Municipal to San Pedro will stop, on demand, at Caye Caulker. Fares are the same as to San Pedro – US$63 one-way from International and from Municipal US$35. Flights from San Pedro to Belize City also drop passengers at Caulker's airstrip, again for the same fare as to Belize City itself.

Most visitors to Caulker, however, come by boat. Two water taxi companies, with fast boats that hold up to 100 passengers, connect Belize City with Caye Caulker (US$7.50 one-way), each with eight to ten departures a day. Caye Caulker Water Taxi Association (www.cayecaulkerwatertaxi.com) boats depart from the Marine Terminal near the Swing Bridge; **San Pedro-Belize Express** aka **San Pedro Water Jets Express** (www.sanpedrowatertaxi.com) boats leave from the nearby Brown Sugar dock near the Tourism Village. It's a 45-minute ride to Caulker.

GETTING ORIENTED

The Caye Caulker Water Taxi Association boats come in at the main public pier on the front side of the island., and the San Pedro Express boats dock at a pier nearby. If you come ashore at the main public pier, the pink and green **Trends Beachfront** hotel and behind it the **Sandbox** restaurant are on your right, and **Seaside Cabañas** are on your left. Walk a few sandy feet and you'll come to Front Street. Go right, or north, and in 10 minutes or so you'll pass several good hotels and end up at the Split. Go left or south and you'll find some of the island's better beachfront properties. Many of the island's restaurants, shops and hotels are on Front Street or on the beachfront.

If you come by air, the little airstrip is at the south end of the island. You can walk the 20 minutes or so back to the heart of the village, or you can get a golf cart taxi.

AGENDA FOR A DAY TRIP TO CAULKER

If you are coming to Caulker as part of a day snorkel tour, you will only have a short time on the island, just enough to walk around and get a sense of the atmosphere.   If you are coming over on an independent day trip, try to get over on an early water taxi, so you'll have time to walk the island and get a good feel for what makes Caulker special.   Caulker isn't a place to do things – there are no museums, few shops and very little formal sightseeing. Instead, it's a place just to hang and to meet some of the friendly *Jicauqueños*. Don't let the few Rastaphonians on the island bother you – just say no if they offer you dope. Take a slow self-guided walking tour of the island, or you can rent a bike or a golf cart.

CAYE CAULKER HOTELS

This is not a complete list of island hotels, but these are among our favorites in all price ranges. They are arranged by location, either north or south of the main "front pier" where the water taxis arrive, and then by price range, from most to least expensive.

North of the Main Front Pier:

★★★ ++ **Caye Reef Condos.** Front St.; tel. 501-226-0381 or 610/0240; www.cayereef.com. Caye Reef Condos are the newest upscale accommodations on the island. The six two-bedroom condo apartments are on Front Street not far from the Split, with a small swimming pool at the front, hidden behind a wall. You can book either a two-bedroom entire unit or just one of the bedrooms. All units are fully air-conditioned, with tile floors, custom kitchens, private verandas with sea views (second and third floors), Belizean art on the walls and flat-screen TVs. There are great views of the reef from the fourth floor roof top patio, where there is a rooftop whirlpool. Rates for the full units are US$195 in-season, US$165 off. The penthouse is US$215 in and US$180 out. Rates plus tax and are higher at Christmas-New Years.

★★★ + **Iguana Reef Inn.** Middle Street next to soccer field, P.O. Box 31, Caye Caulker; tel. 501-226-0213, fax 226-0087; www.iguanareefinn.com. This is the Ritz-Carlton of Caye Caulker. The 12 suites have air-conditioning, Belizean furniture, queen beds and local artwork. A swimming pool was added in late 2006. Considering the size and amenities of the suites, the rates, US$135 to $165 in-season plus tax, are reasonable, and they include continental breakfast. A penthouse suite on the third level with two bedrooms and two baths is pricey at US$375. If there's a downside, it is that the hotel is on the back side of the island and not on the Caribbean, though from some units you have a view of sunsets on the lagoon. The hotel's Web site is a good source of information about the island. No children under 10. The hotel currently is for sale.

★★★++ **Caye Caulker Condos.** Front St., tel. 501-226-0072; www.cayecaulkercondos.com. Want a suite with a full kitchen to prepare some of your own meals? Try these new condo apartments. Each of the 8 cozy units, on the west side of Front Street, has a private veranda facing the water, less than 100 feet away; those on the second floor have the better views. All the units have tile floors and most have satellite TVs, but not phones. Bikes are free. There's now a swimming pool, too. Rates US$120 to $135 double in-season, US$110-$120 off-season, plus 9% hotel tax.

★★+ **De Real Macaw.** Front St.; tel. 501-226-0459, fax 226-0497; www.derealmacaw.biz. This friendly spot, which is on the west side of Front Street but still close enough to catch the breezes, has rooms and a two-bedroom self-catering apartment and beach house, some units with and some without air-conditioning. There's a porch with hammocks. In-season rates:

US$25 to $70 for rooms, US$120-$130 for a two-bedroom unit, slightly lower off-season.

★★ Trends Beachfront Hotel. Beachfront near public pier; tel. 501-226-0094, fax 226-0097; www.trendsbze.com. As you arrive on the water taxi, this tropically pink and green hotel is one of the first things you see, just to the right of the new pier. Thanks to its location and its seven bright clean rooms, each with a queen and a double bed, mini-fridge and private bath, it stays full much of the time. Rates around US$40 double, more if you need A/C. The same people operate the original Trends Guesthouse, around the corner. It's cheaper, but it's not on the water.

★ Tina's Bak Pak Hostel. Beachfront just north of public pier, tel. 501-226-0351; www.tinashostelbelize.com. For US$10 to per person, you can grab a hammock or a bunk bed at this hostel on the beach. Though the original hostel dorms are very basic, you're right on the water, and the price and location mean this place is usually packed with young people. The "penthouse" dorm on the third floor has a nice view of the barrier reef. Tina's Hostel also now runs the former Auxillou Suites next door, which has been converted into upscale hostel space, with bunk beds in air-conditioned comfort at US$25 per person plus tax.

South of the Main Front Pier:

★★★ + Seaside Cabanas. P.O Box 39, Caye Caulker; tel. 501-226-0498, fax 501-226-0125; www.seasidecabanas.com. Rebuilt after a 2003 fire, this seafront hotel, with 15 rooms and a seafront suite, is now one of the top places on the island, and one of the few hotels on the island with a swimming pool. Painted a deep mustard color, with a combination of tropical thatch and Moorish-influenced design, the buildings are in a U-shape. Four of the rooms have private roof-top terraces for sunning or watching the sea in privacy. The hotel now has in-room phones and free Wi-Fi. Rates around USS105 to $130 double most of the year, plus 9% tax. The hotel is currently for sale but is operating normally.

★★★ Tree Tops. P.O. Box 29, Caye Caulker, tel. 501-226-0240, fax 226-0115; www.treetopsbelize.com. Just set back a little from the water, Tree Tops is run by Austrian-born Doris Creasy. All rooms have air-conditioning available, cable TV and a refrigerator. Two third-floor suites (US$98 plus tax), Sunset and Sunrise, have king-size beds and private balconies with views of the water. A small courtyard is a great place to read or just lounge in a hammock. Belize needs more places like this one – the guest rooms are clean as a pin, the entire place is meticulously maintained, the owner is helpful and rooms start around US$50 double. Highly recommended.

★★++ **Barefoot Beach Belize.** tel. 501-226-0205; www.barefootbeachbelize.com. Formerly the Seaview Guest House, the current owners, Kim and Susan Briggs, have turned this little seafront hotel into one of the most popular spots on Caulker. There are three rooms and a suite in a pastel blue, concrete building with pink and yellow trim and three cottages (US$97-$158 a day). Don't confuse this place with the similarly named Barefoot Caribe.

★★++ **Lazy Iguana B&B.** South of the public pier on the back side of the island, near airstrip, tel. 501-226-0350, fax 226-0320; www.lazyiguana.net. Owner Mo Miller says no shoes are required at this four-room B&B. The rooms are furnished with attractive wicker and tropical hardwood furniture. Views of the sunsets from the fourth-level rooftop terrace are terrific. The common room has TV and internet access. Rates US$95 to $105 double year-round, plus tax.

★★+ **Pancho's Villas.** Pasero St., tel. 501-226-0304; www.panchosvillasbelize.com. Pancho's Villas offers six attractive new one-bedroom suites in a yellow three-story building. Each suite has air-conditioning and ceiling fans, cable TV, Wi-Fi, fridge and microwave. It's not on the beach. Rates under US$100 including tax.

★★ **Maxhapan Cabañas.** Tel. 501-226-0118. This little spot is in the center of the village and not on the water, but it's very popular because it's neat and clean and a good value. Set in a small, sandy and shady garden, there are rooms in a two-story cabaña and in a one-level building. They have tile floors and a veranda with hammocks. Complimentary bikes and snorkel gear. Rates around US$80.

★+ Jaguar Morning Star. Middle St. south of the public pier, tel. 501-226-0347; www.jaguarmorningstar.com. This quiet little budget inn, just behind Treetops, is a good value. It's well run by a Belizean-Canadian couple. There are two rooms, way up on the third floor, with a veranda offering views of the island and the sea, plus a little cabin at the back in the garden. Rates US$45 to $65.

★+ Shirley's Guesthouse. South End near nature reserve, P.O. Box 13, Caye Caulker; tel. 501-226-0145; www.shirleysguesthouse.com. Nine cabins and rooms, all clean and pleasant with sea views. Some with shared baths. US$50 to $90 December-May, US$40 to $65 rest of year, plus tax. Adults only.

★ Tom's Hotel. Beachfront, about 4 blocks south of the public

pier, (P.O. Box 15, Caye Caulker), tel. 501-226-0102; e-mail toms@btl.net. This backpacker favorite, with 5 cabins and lots of rooms in a two-story concrete building, continues to attract a crowd. Many rooms are small, share baths and can be very hot, but the seaside location, friendly management and low prices, starting at around US$15, keep regulars coming back. No credit cards.

Vacation Rentals

For small vacation rental house on Caulker, expect to pay around US$350 to $1,000 a week, or US$40 to $100 a night.

Caye Caulker Rentals. Front St., tel. 501-226-0029; www.cayecaulkerrentals.com. This rental agency has some two dozen houses for rent, some from as low as US$50 a night, and others, including beachfront houses, from under US$400 a week.

Heredia's Apartments & House Rentals. Calle del Sol, about a block from the public pier, tel. 501-226-0132. Offers several budget apartments and houses on the lagoon side, most under US$300 a week.

Caye Caulker Dining

Caye Caulker has more than 20 restaurants, mostly small spots with a few tables and sand or wood floors, where you can get a tasty meal for a few dollars. A few are more upmarket. Some don't accept credit cards.

Price ranges shown are for typical meals for one (usually dinner), not including tip, tax or alcoholic drinks. Price ranges:

Inexpensive: Under US$5
Moderate: US$6-$15
Expensive: US$16-30
Very Expensive: Over US$30

Habaneros. Middle Street, tel. 501-226-0486. Caye Caulker's most upscale dining and arguably the best. Try the Snapper Santa Fe. Great fajitas. Mayan Pizza is a speciality for lunch. Moderate to Expensive.

Rose's Grill & Bar. On Center St., the street leading from the main public pier, just behind Haberneros; tel. 501-206-0407. This tiny restaurant is one of the best on the island, and the tables on the porch and inside are often packed. The speciality is seafood, and it's all fresh and delicious. Moderate to Expensive.

Rainbow Grill & Bar. On the beach about halfway between the public pier and the Split, tel. 501-226-0281. The Rainbow is the only eatery on Caye Caulker that's built out over the water, to catch the sea breezes. The grilled or fried seafood dishes are terrific. Inexpensive to Moderate.

Wish Willie's. You eat in the back yard of the chef-owner, Maurice, and he will tell you what's on the menu today. It may be fresh fish, lamb or chicken. In most cases, the prices are low, and the rum drinks cost less here than anywhere else on the island. You may have to share a table with other guests and the service is sometimes slow, but keep in mind the money you're saving. Moderate.

Femi's. Beachfront; tel. 501-622-3469. Popular with younger travelers, Femi's is on the beach, with no walls to spoil the view. The food is pretty good, and the setting is excellent. Moderate.

Sandbox. Front St. at main public pier; tel. 501-226-0200. Whether outside under the palms or indoors under the lazily turning ceiling fans, you'll always have your feet in the sand here. The Sandbox has a large menu, with tasty items such as lobster omelet with fry jacks for breakfast, lobster or conch fritters or barbecue chicken for lunch and red snapper for dinner. At night the bar gets lively. Moderate.

Syd's. Middle Street, south of the public pier, tel. 501-226-0294. Locals often recommend Syd's. It serves Belizean and Mexican faves like beans and rice, stew chicken, garnaches, tostadas along with lobster and conch, when in season, at prices lower than you'll pay at most other eateries. Moderate.

Glenda's. Come to Glenda's for a cinnamon roll, johnnycake and fresh-squeezed orange juice for breakfast, and come back at lunch for rice and beans. Closed for dinner. No credit cards. Inexpensive. **Amor y Cafe** (formerly Cyndi's) is another good place for breakfast, along with love and coffee. Both inexpensive.

Jolly Roger. Front Street near the Health Center. At little tables beside his house, Roger serves some of the best lobster on the island, at bargain prices.   He barbecues delicious fish, too. Moderate.

WHERE TO PARTY

For Belikin and booze, the **Lazy Lizard** at the Split is among the most popular bars on the island. Its slogan is "A sunny place for shady people." For live music, your best bet is **Oceanside** on Front St. near the main public pier. **I&I,** near Tropical Paradise, a funky joint with rope swings and hammocks instead

A sandy side street in Caye Caulker village

of chairs, blows reggae and other music. In the back is a tree house. **Popeye's** and **Sandbox** also are popular places to soothe a thirst. **Herbal Tribe** is near the Spit is a reggae bar.

DIVING, SNORKELING, FISHING, TOURS

From Caye Caulker, you dive and snorkel most of the same spots you do from San Pedro, though prices for snorkel trips and diving may be slightly less. If you are staying in San Pedro, the difference in dive prices probably isn't enough to warrant a special trip to Caulker, although for dive instruction, the price difference can be significant, with a complete course starting at about US$250. Many boats offer reef snorkeling trips, starting at about US$20 for snorkeling around Caye Caulker. If you want to snorkel Hol Chan Marine Reserve near San Pedro, you'll pay US$40 to $50 for a six-hour trip, usually including entrance fee to the park, lunch and rum punch.

Local one-tank dives run about US$55, two-tank reef dives typically run about US$80 and those to Hol Chan or other nearby areas, about US$90 to $100.   Day trips to Lighthouse or Turneffe Atolls, with three dives, cost around US$120 to $200.

You can go for a snorkel on a sailboat with **Raggamuffin Tours** (tel. 501-226-0348; www.raggamuffintours.com, which goes to Hol Chan for US$45 including the park entrance fee, lunch and rum punch. **Tsunami Adventures (**tel. 501-226-0462; www.tsunamiadventures.com) has snorkeling trips to Hol Chan for US$45 including the park entrance fee and lunch, and a local Caye Caulker reef trip for US$25. **Carlos Tours** (tel. 501-226-0058) also does snorkel trips. Red Mangrove Eco Adventures (Front St.; tel. 501-226-0069) ecologically sensitive snorkel and mainland trips - no touching the sharks.

If you're looking for someone to take you out to the reef or to Turneffe for diving, **Frenchie's Diving Services (**tel. 501-226-0234) is a good local operator. Another is **Belize Diving Services** (tel. 501-226-0143). Paradise Down is no longer operating.

Among the best known and most recommended guides on the island is the famous **Captain Chocolate** (tel. 501-226-0151; e-mail chocolate@btl.net). **Ras Creek** does a popular trip to the reef and around the island, complete with lunch and rum punch, for around US$20.

SHOPPING AND SERVICES

If you thought San Pedro shopping was limited, wait until you get to Caye Caulker. Aside from a few gift shops, there's little here on which to spend your money. **Caribbean Colors** (Front St., tel. 501-226/2206) has watercolors and silk screenings by the owner, Lee Vanderwalker-Kroll, along with handmade jewelry, scarves and art by other artists. **Coopers Art Gallery** on Front St., tel. 501-226-0330, has paintings and prints by Walter Castillo and other Central American artists, along with pieces by owner Debbie Cooper. For groceries, probably **Chan's Mini-Mart,** down from the public pier, is the largest. For medical care, a doctor and nurse are on duty at the **Medical Clinic** (tel.

Trends Hotel on Caye Caulker

501-226-0166). **Atlantic Bank** now has an ATM that accepts foreign-issued ATM cards.

For More Information

Several web sites have good information on Caye Caulker: The official **Caye Caulker Village Council** web site (www.cayecaulkerbelize.net) has lots of information on island history, people and activities. It lists many island businesses.

Another "official" site is Go Caye Caulker (www.gocayecaulker.com), put up by the **Caye CaulkerBelize Tourism Association**. CayeCaulker.org (www.cayecaulker.org) is affiliated with Marty Casado's Ambergriscaye.com site.

Belize's Other Islands

Belize's two northern cayes, Ambergris and Caulker, are the two largest and by far the most popular of Belize's island, both by expats and visitors. However, Belize has more than 400 other islands in the Caribbean. Most are small, remote and unpopulated. They are wonderful if typically somewhat expensive to visit. Here, briefly, are some of the options for lodging.

ST. GEORGE'S CAYE

Historical St. George's Caye is only about 8 miles or 20 minutes by boat from Belize City. It was the site of perhaps the most famous event in Belize history, when, as the story goes, in September 1798 a ragtag group of Baymen defeated a larger Spanish fleet from Mexico. St. George's Caye Day on September 10 celebrates the culminating Belizean victory. Today, St. George's Caye is home to one dive resort and to a number of weekend and holiday homes of Belize City's economic elite.

St. George's Caye Resort. St. George's Caye; tel. 800-813-8498; www.gooddiving.com. This long-established resort, focused on diving and fishing, has 12 cabañas, including some that are set over the water, and a main lodge building. It's the exact opposite of a large resort. You get personal attention here and sometimes you may be the only guests at the hotel. However, prices are high - around US$500 a day or more per couple including taxes and service and not including high-cost items like fishing and diving -- and the new management does not always get positive feedback from guests. All-inclusive rates are US$197 to $279 per person in-season and US$197 to $246 per person off-season. Rates are plus tax and 10% service charge, and do NOT include diving or fishing, but do include lodging, all meals, transfers from the international airport (with 4-night booking), domestic bar beverages and alcohol, unlimited use of kayaks, hobie cats, windsurfers and snorkeling gear.

SPANISH LOOKOUT CAYE

Hugh Parkey's Belize Adventure Lodge. Spanish Lookout Caye (P.O. Box 1818, Belize City); tel. 501-223-452; www.belizeadventurelodge.com. Named after a well-known dive and hotel operator in Belize City who with his wife Therese ran the famous Fort Street Guesthouse. He died in 2002. This lodge formerly featured a swim-with-dolphins program. Now it has 12 cabañas on a 186-acre island about 25 minutes from Belize City. Some of the cabañas are built over water. Rates are attractive, US$200 double year-round, including meals. Transfer from Belize City is US$38.50. Four-night dive packages, including transfers, lodging in an over-the-water cabaña, meals and four

dives is US$1,249 per person in winter and US$1,099 per person in summer.

RAGGED CAYE RANGE

★★★★ **Royal Belize.** Ragged Caye Range; tel. 305-675-4660; www.royalbelize.com. This private resort on a 7 1/2-acre caye is a 30-minute boat ride from Dangriga. There are just four cottages on the island, which rent from US$350 a night, but at that rate there may be other guests on the island, or from US$600 to $1150 a night on an exclusive basis, if you want the island to yourself (even if you only rent one house). Minimum three-day stays, and taxes are additional. All on-island activities are included in the rates, including use of a Wave Runner, kayaks and snorkeling equipment. Diving, fishing and land tours are not included, nor are meals or drinks. Custom meals (US$50 per person per day) are prepared according to the guests' preferences. Booze is at cost plus 20%.

TOBACCO CAYE

About 10 miles east of Dangriga, Tobacco Caye is a tiny 5-acre coral island. It is getting more attention these days because it offers snorkeling off the shore. As so often happens in Belize, though, rates have shot up at some of the hotels here. There's no scheduled water taxi service, but you can hook a boat at Dangriga to take you out – around US$17.50 one-way. Captain Buck is reliable. Check at the Riverside Café.

★+ **Tobacco Caye Lodge.** Tel. 501-520-5033; www.tclodgebelize.com. About the best the island has to offer, with tropically blue duplex cabins. Double rooms are around US$80.

★ **Gaviota Coral Reef Resort.** Tel. 501-509-5032. The food here, served family-style at fixed times, is very good. You'll enjoy fresh fish, beans and rice, and even salads. The clapboard rooms and cabins are tiny, but the location on the east side of the caye provides cooling breezes. A new cabin is built over the water. At under US$40 per person, plus tax, including all meals, it's a good value.

Other choices: ★ + **Reef's End. ★ Lana's on the Reef, ★ Paradise** and ★ **Ocean's End.**

SOUTHWATER CAYE MARINE RESERVE

Southwater Caye, about 15 acres in size, is one of the most beautiful small islands off Belize. The south end of the caye, where Pelican Beach's cottages are located, has a nice little beach and snorkeling right off the shore.

★★★ + **Pelican Pouch.** P.O. Box 2, Dangriga; tel. 501-522-2044, fax 522-2570; www.southwatercaye.com. Three charming but simple cottages plus five budget rooms in the main building. In-season, cottages are US$220 double including three meals; rooms are US$165 with all meals. Rates include tax. For around US$500 a person, Pelican Beach also has a four-night package – three nights at South Water and one night at its hotel in Dangriga, including meals, boat to South Water and taxes.

Other choices on the island is the expensive ★★★ **Blue Marlin Lodge** (501-520-2243, www.bluemarlinlodge.com), with good dive and fishing options, and the budget-level ★ **International Zoological Expeditions Cottages** (501-520-5030, www.ize2belize.com), which caters to student groups.

Note: Visitors to Southwater Caye Marine Reserve (including those staying on Tobacco Caye and Southwater Caye) pay US$5 a day per person marine reserve fee, or US$15 for up to a week's stay.

Cocoplum Range

These islands are about 9 miles off Dangriga. They are not directly on the reef.

★★★★ **Thatch Caye.** P.O. Box 143, Dangriga; tel. 501-603-2414 or toll-free 800-435-3145; www.thatchcayebelize.com. There are 11 guest cottages on this "hand built" island. (The owners spent years putting up bamboo sea walls and raised boardwalks.) You can head out for a day of fishing, diving, sea kayaking, or snorkeling, then enjoy a delicious meal in the thatched dining room, sip an ice-cold drink and surf the web on the free Wi-Fi in the bar before heading to your seaside cabaña or casita where you'll be lulled asleep by the tradewinds (air conditioning is available in some units for US$50 a day extra).

Some of the cabañas are built partly over water, while the slightly more expensive casitas have third-level "widow walks" where you can gaze for hours at the sea. In-season weekly packages including lodging, all meals, snorkel and mainland trips and transportation from Dangriga are around US$2,800 to $3,600 double. Thatch Caye strives for sustainability, with solar and wind power.

★★★ **Coco Plum Caye.** This 16-acre island has five cottages, all air-conditioned and painted in bright tropical colors. All-inclusive rates include meals, drinks and use of snorkeling equipment and kayaks, with a minimum four-night stay. The snorkeling off the shore is only so-so, but most rates include snorkel trips to the reef a few miles farther out. Diving and fishing packages also available. Rates: Around US$500 a night double, all-inclusive.

Whipray Caye

Whipray Caye, about 11 miles off Placencia, is a great spot for anglers, as you can wade out about 50 yards in the flats and fish for tarpon, permit and other gamefish. Julian Cabral, a well-known Placencia fishing guide, owns the island and with American wife Beverly Montgomery-Cabral operates ★★ **Whipray Lodge** and the **Sea Urchin** bar and restaurant (tel. 501-610-1068, www.whipraycayelodge.com.) The three basic cabins can accommodate up to eight people. There's also good snorkeling here.

THE ATOLLS

Atolls are characterized by a large lagoon surrounded by coral reefs. While atolls are common in the South Pacific, they are rare in the Western Hemisphere. Of the four known atolls in the Western Hemisphere, three are in Belize – Glovers, Turneffe and Lighthouse. (The fourth, Chinchorra, is in southern Mexico,)

GLOVERS ATOLL

Glovers Atoll is the smallest of the three atolls in Belize, with an area of about 140 square miles. Some 45 miles from the mainland, Glovers offers some of the best diving and snorkeling in the Caribbean. The atoll has hundreds of coral patches in the lagoon. Around the atoll are 50 miles of walls dropping from 40 to 2500 feet or more. Fishing is restricted in this marine reserve – if you are fishing, reserve rangers will collect a fee of US$10 per person per day. Salt-water fishing licenses now are required. *See page 75 for information.*

★★★ **Isla Marisol.** 189A Rear Ghans Ave., Dangriga; el. 501-615-1485 or 501-520-2056; www.islamarisol.com. Southwest Caye, where Isla Marisol is located, is owned by the Usher family, which obtained the island in the 1940s. Lodging at this resort is mostly in small wood cabins with zinc roofs. There's a restaurant and bar. Three-night beachcomber packages, including lodging, meals and transport from Belize City, start at about US$2,000 per couple from November to June and US$1,900 the rest of the year. Fishing and dive packages are higher.

★★ + **Off the Wall Dive Center and Resort.** Long Caye, tel. 501-614-6348; www.offthewallbelize.com. Run by Kendra and Jim Schofield, Off the Wall focuses on diving, but there's excellent snorkeling and fishing as well. Facilities are rustic — small wood cabins, composting toilets, and outdoor rainwater showers. Meals are served in a beachfront thatch palapa with sand floor. There is no a/c, no room phones, no room TVs, which many find just about perfect. Rates US$1,395 to $2,095 per person weekly, depending on activities.

★ **Glovers Atoll Resort.** P.O. Box 563, Belize City; tel. 501-520-5016, fax 501-223-6087; www.glovers.com.bz. Don't let the name mislead you – this isn't your typical resort. The Lomont family, who came to Belize in the 1960s, offer very basic accommodations on Northeast Caye, about 45 miles out in the Caribbean at a reasonable price in a beautiful setting. You won't get running water or electricity here, but you can enjoy one of the most stunning parts of the Caribbean Sea. Around the 9-acre island you can dive or snorkel right from the shore. Weekly per-person rates year-round: Simple palmetto thatch cabañas are US$249 and those built over the water are US$299; thatch cabañas on beach, US$249; dorm room or tent, US$199; camping, US$149. Children under 12 are half price. Rates include transportation by boat to and from Sittee River near Hopkins but not 9% hotel tax. A weekly boat from Sittee River leaves Sundays. You'll need to bring most everything you need, including toilet paper, food, beer, cooler with ice and other supplies. Bottled water (US$1.50 a gallon) and kerosene (US$1 a pint) and a few grocery items are usually available on the island. Simple meals are offered, but they're fairly expensive – breakfast US$9, lunch US$12, dinner US$18-22. You can rent kayaks, canoes, and dive and snorkel gear. All in all Glovers Atoll Resort is quite a remarkable place, but not for everyone.

LIGHTHOUSE REEF ATOLL

Lighthouse Atoll is about 45 miles off the mainland coast, east of Belize City. The atoll is famous (thanks to Jacques Cousteau, for the Blue Hole inside the lagoon. The Blue Hole, an underwater sinkhole or cenote, is about one-quarter mile across and about 500 feet deep. Divers usually find the Blue Hole less interesting than they expected it would be, with very little sea life other than some sharks, but it's worth doing once. Several divers have died here, and it is not for novice divers. Half Moon Caye, a 45-acre coral island, is one of the most beautiful of all the Belize cayes, and it was part of Belize's first marine reserve. There's a daily fee of US$40 per person to visit the reserve.

Lighthouse Reef Resort is closed for renovation and may eventually reopen under a new name. You may be able to arrange accommodatons at Long Caye. Try **Calypso Beach Retreat** (303-523-8165; www.calypsobeachretreat.com), which is open when there is demand from dive groups.

TURNEFFE ATOLL

Turneffe Atoll is about 25 miles from the mainland, to the east of Belize City. The central lagoon, which has some 200 small mangrove islands, is about 240 square miles in area. There is also a smaller northern lagoon. Like Belize's other atolls, Turneffe offers magnificent diving and great fishing. The eastern and southern side of the atoll offers the best diving. Probably the most famous site is The Elbow, on the southern tip. Spur and groove diving is here only for experienced divers.

★★★+ **Turneffe Flats.** U.S. office: P.O. Box 36, Deadwood, SD 57732; tel. 800-815-1304 or 605-578-1304, fax 605-578-7540; www.tflats.com. It's remote, it's beautiful and it's air-conditioned. The lodge, on the northeast side of the atoll, provides boat transport from Belize City to Turneffe on Saturdays. The trip takes about 90 minutes. Dive packages are around

US$2,250-$2,500 per person for a week, depending on the time of yearinclusive of lodging, meals, three dives a day and transport to the island but not booze, tips or taxes. Weekly fishing packages are more, around US$3,500 to $4,000 per person. Shorter packages are available at some times.

★★★ **Blackbird Caye Resort.** tel. 1-888-271-3483; www.blackbirdresort.com. Owned by a well-connected Belizean family, Blackbird Caye (currently for sale) , on the eastern side of the atoll, is another option on beautiful Turneffe. All units have air-conditioning. The newer deluxe cabins are more spacious, with king beds. Dinner is served in a large thatch palapa. Dive packages from around US$1,100 per person for three days, US$2,300 per person weekly, per person, in high season, slightly less off-season.

★★★ **Turneffe Island Resort.** U.S. office: 440 Louisiana, Ste. 300, Houston, TX 77002; tel. 800-874-0118 or 713-236-7739, fax 713-236-7743; www.turnefferesort.com. Accommodations are in eight private cabañas or in 20 rooms in four buildings on Big Caye Bokel at the southern end of the central lagoon. Three-night packages range from US$800 to $2,500 per person, depending on the time of year, level of accommodations and the type of activities.

Bonus Section
LIVING, RETIRING, INVESTING AND BUYING PROPERTY IN BELIZE

Even if you're a world traveler with a bazillion frequent-flier miles, chances are that you'll be fascinated by your first glimpses of Belize. Hundreds of travel-poster islands dot the turquoise sea along Belize's 200-mile coast, with Ambergris Caye being the largest and most developed. Just offshore is the longest barrier reef in the Northern and Western hemispheres, with an undersea world of fantastic color and diversity. The diving and snorkeling are world-class, and the fishing is so good that it usually takes just a few minutes to catch a snapper or spiny lobster for your lunch.

Inland are lightly populated savannas, limestone hills and lush rainforests, home to more than 500 species of birds, 800 kinds of butterflies and 4,000 varieties of trees and shrubs. Bananas and mangos grow like weeds. Exotic animals like the jaguar and tapir still roam free in "backabush" Belize. Hidden under cohune palms are thousands of mysterious Maya ruins. The small villages and towns of Belize are alive with a cultural gumbo of colors, races and backgrounds.

But Belize also appeals to those who want to linger longer than a week or two of vacation in paradise. It is getting the attention of prospective retirees and relocatees who want a laid-back lifestyle in a frost-free climate similar to South Florida, with a stable government and economy, and a familiar legal system based on English common law where all documents are written in English.

Retirees are attracted by relatively low real estate costs and an overall cost of living that stretches retirement pensions and Social Security checks farther than they would go in the United States. But most of all they like friendly Belizean neighbors who usually put out a subtropical welcome mat for Americans.

"This is the friendliest place I have ever been, and I have traveled a lot. Belizeans take people one at a time – foreign or local is not the issue. How you behave and how you are in your heart is what makes the difference," says Diane Campbell, a real estate developer and builder on Ambergris Caye who moved to Belize from California. "If you are nice, kind and honest, you will be loved and respected here. When you get used to living here, you won't be able to imagine living elsewhere."

OPTIONS FOR LIVING IN BELIZE

There are three options for those wishing to live or retire in Belize or to spend extended periods of time in the country. Each has advantages and disadvantages.

TOURIST CARD

This is the easiest, cheapest way to live in the country for a while, and it requires no long-term commitment.   The procedure is simple: You get a 30-day entry free (via a passport stamp) when you arrive in the country by air, land or sea. After 30 days, you can go to an immigration office (or police station in remote areas) and renew the tourist card monthly for US$25 a month for up to six months, and then US$50 a month after that.   After six months, you also must register as an alien. Citizens of the U.S., European Community, the U.K., Canada, Australia, New Zealand, Mexico, Costa Rica, Guatemala, Suriname, Fiji, Hungary, Iceland, Kenya, Latvia, Lithunania, Seychelles, South Africa, Singapore, Slovakia, Soloman Islands, Malawi, Malaysia, Maldives, Mauritius, Czech Republic, Namibia, Papua New Guinea, Chile, Norway, Sierra Leone, Sweden, Tanzania, Turkey, Uganda, Uruguay, Zambia, Western Samoa, Zimbabwe, Tuvalu, Venezuela, Hong Kong, CARICOM member states and some other countries get a tourist card without having to apply in advance for a tourist visa. Nationals of more than 75 other countries must apply in advance for a tourist visa, and there is a fee. See the Belize Tourism Board web site, www.travelbelize.org for details.

As a tourist cardholder, you can enjoy Belize without a long-term commitment. You can buy or rent property, but you cannot work for pay. In theory, when you renew your tourist card, you are supposed to be able to prove that you have sufficient resources, set at US$60 a day, to stay in Belize, but this requirement is not usually enforced. Of course, there is no guarantee that you will be able to renew your card indefinitely, as rules and conditions can change, as you have no official residency status. If you fail to renew your permit in a timely way, or if you overstay your allotted time, technically you are in violation of Belize law and can be deported. As a practical matter, if you can offer a good reason why you failed to follow the law, and are very friendly to Immigration officers, you'll probably be let off with a short lecture from the official, and perhaps a fine. However, some people who overstay their tourist cards *are* sent packing.

QUALIFIED RETIRED PERSON STATUS

The Qualified Retired Persons Incentive Act passed by the Belize legislature in 1999 is being implemented by the Belize Tourism Board. The program is designed to attract more retirees to Belize. In the first years of operation, the program attracted considerable interest and a number of applications. But the Belize Tourism Board doesn't disclose how many applications it has received and how many have been approved. However, we understand that there are only several hundred active participants in the program. Interest in the program appears to be fairly high, but because of the income requirement, inability to work for pay in Belize and other factors, the actual number of retirees under the program in Belize is as yet relatively small and far fewer than are in programs in Costa Rica, Panama, Mexico and elsewhere. The program is being reviewed by the BTB to see if it can be made more competitive.

For those who can show the required monthly income from investments or pensions, this program offers benefits of official residency and tax-free entry of the retiree's household goods and a car, boat and even an airplane. This program also eliminates some of the bureaucratic delays built into other programs. The BTB guarantees action on an application in no more than three months, but we have heard of qualified retirees getting approval for this program in only a few weeks.

Who qualifies? Anyone at least 45 years old from anywhere in the world can qualify for the program. A person who qualifies can also include his or her dependents in the program. Dependents include spouses and children under the age of 18. However, it can include children under the age of 23 if enrolled in a university.

Main benefits: Besides prompt approval of residency for qualifying applicants, import duties and fees for household goods and a vehicle, airplane and boat are waived.

Duty-free import of personal household effects: Qualified Retired Persons under the program can qualify for duty and tax exemptions on new and used personal and household effects admitted as such by the Belize Tourism Board. A list of all items with corresponding values that will be imported must be submitted with the application. A one-year period is granted for the importation of personal and household effects.

Duty-free import of a vehicle, aircraft and boat:

a. Motor Vehicle: Applicants are encouraged to import new motor vehicles under the program, but the vehicle must be no more than three years old. (An exception may be made in the case of an older vehicle with low mileage, but this would be decided on a case-by-case basis.) A Qualified Retired Person may also buy a vehicle duty-free in country.

b. Light Aircraft: A Qualified Retired Person is entitled to import a light aircraft less than 17,000 kg. A Qualified Retired Person is required to have a valid Private Pilot license to fly in Belize. This license can be obtained by passing the requirements set by the Civil Aviation. However, if the participant has a valid pilot's license, that license only has to be validated by Civil Aviation Department in Belize.

c. Boat: Any vessel that is used for personal purposes and for pleasure will be accepted under this program. If for whatever reason a Qualified Retired Person decides to sell, give away, lease, or otherwise dispose of the approved means of transportation or personal effects to any person or entity within Belize, all duties and taxes must be paid to the proper authorities. The Belize Tourism Board states: "Qualified Retired Persons must note that only after three years and upon proof that the transportation that was previously imported to Belize was adequately disposed off, will another concession be granted to import another mode of transportation."

Income requirement: To be designated a Qualified Retired Person under the program, the applicant must have a monthly income of at least US$2,000. A couple does not need to show US$4,000 a month – just US$2,000, as the applicant is normally an individual and the applicant's spouse is a dependent under the program. The income rules for Qualified Retired Persons are, like many things in Belize, a little confusing. On first reading, it looks like the income must derive from a pension or annuity that has been generated outside of Belize. The rules do not specifically say so, but according to Belize Tourism Board offi-cials U.S. Social Security income can be included as part of this pension requirement. This pension and annuity information then has to be substantiated by a Certified Public Accountant, along with two bank references from the company providing the pen-sion or annuity. These substantiations may not be required if your pension and/or annuity is from a Fortune 500 company. Several retirees have told me that they were able to include other forms of income, including investment income, in the US$2,000 figure, if supported by a CPA's statement that the income would continue indefinitely. In this latter case, the US$2,000 a month income (US$24,000 a year) can be substan-tiated by showing records from a bank or other financial institu-tion in Belize that the retiree has deposited the necessary money.

Background check: All applications are subject to a background check by the Ministry of National Security.

Application: Applications for the program must be made to the Belize Tourism Board in Belize City and include the following:

   • Birth certificate: A certified copy of a certificate for the applicant and each dependant.

   • Marriage certificate if applicant is married and spouse is a dependant.

   • Police record: A police record from the applicant's last

place of residency issued within one month prior to the application

• Passport: Color copies of complete passport (including all blank pages) of applicant and all dependents that have been certified by a Notary Public. The copies must have the passport number, name of principal, number of pages and the seal or stamp of the Notary Public.

• Proof of income: An official statement from a bank or financial institution certifying that the applicant is the recipient of a pension or annuity of a minimum of US$2,000 per month.

• Medical examination: Applicants should undergo a complete medical examination including an AIDS test. A copy of the medical certificate must be attached to the application.

• Photos: Four front and four-side passport size photographs that have been taken recently of applicant and dependents.

The application form for the Qualified Retired Persons Program is available for download on the Belize Tourism Board Website at www.belizeretirement.org. Application fees and costs for the QRP program total US$1,350 for an individual or US$2,100 for a couple.

For information on the program, contact: Belize Tourism Board, P.O. Box 325, Belize City, Belize, Central America; tel: 501-223-1913 or 1-800-624-0686; fax: 501-223-1943. If you have questions or problems, try contacting the Program Officer. The current Program Officer is Romy Haylock (email romy@travelbelize.org). She is very helpful.

Note that the BTB currently is reviewing possible changes and improvements in the QRP program. Stay tuned.

OFFICIAL PERMANENT RESIDENT

Application requirements and most benefits are similar to those of the Retired Persons Incentive Act, but there are some important differences. The application process itself and the supporting documents needed are similar to those for the QRP, although the applications are processed by different organizations.

Here are the main differences: As a regular permanent resident, you have two major advantages over a participant in the QRP program. First, you do not have to deposit any particular sum in a bank in Belize. However, you do have to show financial resources sufficient to obtain residency status.   Second, as a permanent resident, you can work for pay in Belize. You also enjoy some advantages as a resident rather than a "long-term visitor" as you are considered as a QRPer, such as not having to pay the land or sea exit tax when departing Belize. As a permanent resident, you can vote in local (not national) Belize elections.

You must live in Belize for one full year before you can apply for regular permanent residency. During this period, you cannot leave the country for more than 14 days. Even a short, two-hour visit to Chetumal counts as one day's absence.   Note, however, that the Immigration and Nationality Department sometimes interprets this requirement only as meaning that you cannot leave the country for 14 or more CONSECUTIVE days.

Here are the documents you must have to apply for permanent residency (photocopies of original documents must be submitted along with the original documents):

• Application form.

• Passport.

• Evidence, such as passport pages with immigration stamps, that you have been in the country for one year.

• Recent police record for yourself and all members of your family over the age of 16.

• Evidence you have acquired property in Belize if you are claiming that you have – but owning property in Belize is NOT required to obtain permanent residency.

• Alien registration for yourself and all members of your family if you have resided in Belize for six months or longer.

• Certificate of health including HIV and venereal disease tests for you and all members of your family – these tests must be conducted in Belize.

• Three passport-size photos of yourself and all members of your family.

• Birth certificates of all applicants.

• Marriage certificate (if applicable).

• Recent local bank statement if means of financial support is not otherwise demonstrated.

• Temporary work permit if you are planning to work for pay.

• Income tax statement.

After approval, you have up to one year to bring in household effects duty-free, on a one-time basis. However, the duty-free exemption does not apply to a vehicle, boat and airplane, as it does for the Qualified Retired Persons program.

It is somewhat expensive to apply for regular permanent residency. Application fees for Permanent Residency vary by nationality, ranging from US$250 to $5,000. For Americans, the fee is US$1,000 per person. There is also, upon approval, a fee of US$150. In addition, if you use an "expediter" in Belize to help you with the paperwork, you'll likely pay a fee of around US$1,500, plus several hundred dollars in travel and photocopying fees and taxes. Note that these fees are per-person, not per-application, as is the case for the Qualified Retired Persons program. For example, an American married couple applying for permanent residency would pay US$2,000 with the application and US$300 for residency cards after approval. Some applicants also have been required to post a bond, supposedly to guarantee the cost of repatriation to their home country, should that ever be required. The bond amount varies, ranging from several hundred dollars to as much as US$2,000. Other applicants say they have not been required to post the bond. Residency cards are no longer provided — instead, your passport is stamped.

You apply to the Belize Immigration and Nationality Department rather than through the Belize Tourism Board. For information and application form, contact: Immigration and Nationality Department Ministry of National Security and Immigration, Belmopan City, Belize, Central America; tel.: 501-222-4620; fax: 501-222-4056.

Time for approval of a permanent residency application varies. Some find that the process goes fairly quickly, taking only a few months. Others say it took up to a year, or longer, for approval.

Pros and Cons
Each option has pluses and minuses. The main advantages and disadvantages are:

Tourist Card
Pros: No commitment, no financial requirement, flexibility, little red tape.

Cons: No tax advantages, no official status, inconvenience of having to renew periodically, monthly fee of US$25 to $50 per person to extend, possibility rules may change, can't work for pay in Belize.

Qualified Retired Persons Incentive Program
Pros: Quick approval, application through Belize Tourism Board rather than Immigration Department, some residency rights (except voting), tax-free entry of household effects, car, boat and airplane, only have to live in country for one month a year.

Cons: Must deposit US$24,000 a year in a Belize bank, somewhat costly application process, can't work for pay in Belize, must be 45 or over, still have to pay tourist exit taxes when leaving the country.

Official Permanent Residency
Pros: Full residency rights (except voting in national elections — you can vote in local elections), can work, open to anyone regardless of age, tax-free entry of household effects.

Cons: Year-long residency before applying, more red tape, costly application process, and some people are turned down for minor details; you can bring in household goods but NOT a car, boat or airplane free of duty.

The controversial Economic Citizenship program, under which foreigners were able to buy a Belize passport and residency rights for a fee of US$25,000 to $50,000, was discontinued in 2002.

In addition to these programs, regular citizenship in Belize is a possibility for those living in Belize over a long period. To acquire citizenship, applicants must have been a resident or have permanent residency status for a minimum of five years. Applicants for citizenship need to provide essentially the same supporting documentation as those applying for permanent residency. Applicants also must demonstrate a knowledge of Belizean history. Note that for citizenship residency purposes, stays in the Belize under the Qualified Retired Persons program do NOT qualify. To become a citizen, you would have to give up QRP status (perhaps having to pay back the duties you escaped under QRP), apply for permanent residency, and begin the five-year residency from scratch.

Caution: Rules and regulations and the interpretation of them change frequently in Belize. Do NOT assume that this information is the last word on any matter pertaining to entering or staying in Belize.

BELIZE IS NOT FOR EVERYONE

Whether they come to Belize under the new retirement program or not, retirees say they like living in a country with many of the conveniences of modern life, such as internet connections, air-conditioning and North American-style houses, but without franchised fast-food restaurants and chain stores that have come to dominate America's frenetic consumer culture. Belize has no Wal-Marts or McDonald's restaurants.

Belize is not for everybody, however. "We've seen so many gringos give up and go home, and so many others still here who are burned out and bitter, that you sometimes feel there is really something insidious underlying the friendly surface appearances," says an ex-Coloradan who runs a jungle lodge in western Belize.

"You have to really like Belize for what it is. You must be prepared to adapt your lifestyle to fit Belize – Belize will not adapt to you," says Pamella Picon, formerly co-owner of Mopan River Resort in Benque Viejo del Carmen.

For those who are willing to put up with the challenges – such as lack of high-tech medical care, a high crime rate in some areas, the high cost of imported items and the occasional hurricane – Belize can be a wonderful place to live.

With a big SUV in the driveway and Belize gasoline approaching over US$5 a gallon, the Carrier turned to frigid and three fingers of Jack Black in the glass, living in Belize can cost more than back home. But if you live as a local – eating the same foods Belizeans do, using public transport and living in a Belizean-style home with ceiling fans and cooling breezes – you can get by on a few hundred dollars per month. Writer and iconoclast Ray Auxillou says he and his wife, who live in Santa Elena in Cayo District, get by on less than US$600 a month, though they own their own home and so don't have to pay rent. A middle-aged expat in Corozal says she rent a nice small house

171

for US$250 a month. A couple in Caye Caulker, who own their own home, say their monthly budget is around US$1,000. Combining some elements of both American and Belizean lifestyles, you can live well for less than you would pay back home. Health care, the cost of renting, buying or building a home in most areas, personal and auto insurance, property taxes, household labor and most products produced in Belize are less expensive than what you're used to paying.

For many, living in Belize is cheaper than in the United States. "I need neither heating nor air-conditioning with their attendant bills, nor insulation in my house, nor much of a house, nor much in the way of shoes. One casual wardrobe serves all purposes except travel back to the USA," one expat says.

If you know where to look, prices for seaview or rural real estate in Belize will remind you of costs in the United States in the 1970s. In small towns in Belize, you can rent a pleasant house near the sea for US$300 to $800 a month, possibly less. Land in larger tracts can sell for US$300 an acre or less. Outside of high-cost tourist areas, you can build for US$35-$75 per square foot or buy an attractive, modern home for US$75,000-$200,000. Property taxes in Belize are low, rarely over $100-$200 annually even for a luxury home.

Despite the relatively high cost of food and electricity, and the pricey island real estate, the overall cost of living on Ambergris Caye (and on Caye Caulker) is lower than in the U.S., say many residents. In part, that's because you don't need all the things you do in the U.S. – no heating oil, no cars or auto insurance or parking fees, and no fancy wardrobe. Seafood and Belize-produced food are comparatively inexpensive. Medical care, cable television, property taxes and basic telephone service, though not international long distance, are among the items which are cheaper than back home.

In one way, island residents can save a lot of money: There's little need for a car or high-priced gas. A number of San Pedranos have brought cars to the island, too many for the limited infrastructure, spurring a moratorium on permits for cars, but few expat island residents have cars. Instead they usually depend on golf carts, which are available used on the island starting for around US$2,000.

People choose Belize as a place to live, year-round or part-time, for a variety of reasons, most associated with the laidback lifestyle, warm subtropical climate and access to the outdoors and the Caribbean. Island life, however, presents its own special set of pleasures and problems. On Ambergris Caye, residents say island fever strikes from time to time. Most residents go into Belize City regularly to conduct business, shop for items not available on the island or to get dental care. Many expats take vacations in the U.S., or long weekends in Cayo district or elsewhere in Belize.

If you aren't busy selling real estate or running a hotel, the island offers some volunteer opportunities. Some expats help out at the local library, or do church work (the island has one Catholic church and several Protestant denominations). The San Pedro chapter of the Lions Club is the island's most active civic organization. Its weekly barbecue on Friday and Saturday nights is delicious, cheap and a fund-raiser for the group's good works.

For those who can't find enough to occupy themselves, substance abuse is always a risk, more so in San Pedro's freewheeling resort atmosphere than in most other areas of Belize. "Booze is ubiquitous here, and bar-hanging quite the social custom. And, in San Pedro as much as in most U.S. cities, you can now add other chemicals. If you're vulnerable, unimaginative, not a self-starter, passive-dependent, maybe Peoria would be a better bet," says one American who lived on the island for many years.

In the past, expats used to say that their hospitals were TACA, American and Continental airlines. For top-flight medical care, Americans on the island may still fly to Miami or Houston, or at least pop over to Belize City, but there are now full-time physicians on the island, along with a clinic operated by the local Lions Club.

Most residents say they feel safe on the island. Burglary and petty thefts are relatively common, and most expats will have a home break-in sooner or later, but violent crime is relatively rare.

A tax affecting expatriate residents is the national 10% Goods and Services tax on nearly everything, with exclusions for some food and medical items. Import taxes are a primary source of government revenue. They vary but can range up to 80% of the value of imported goods. Official residents in Belize under the Retired Persons Incentive Act do not have to pay import duties on a car, boat, plane and up to US$15,000 in household goods imported into the country. For those working for pay in Belize, the country has a progressive personal income tax with a top personal rate of 25%. Belize has no estate or capital gains tax. On real estate purchases, buyers currently must pay a 5% transfer fee, rolled back in mid-2006 from 15% formerly paid by non-citizens. The 10% GST applies to purchases of new condos, new homes and lots in a subdivision, but it does not apply to purchases of an existing house or a small piece of land.

Daily Life on the Islands

What's daily life like on the islands? Of course, it varies from person to person in Belize as it does anywhere in the world. But here's a composite picture of a typical week in the life of an expat couple living in San Pedro.

Monday
You get up around 6 a.m. and watch the sun rise over the Caribbean, while enjoying your regular breakfast of fresh fruit and coffee. This morning it's bananas and watermelon. The bananas cost about 10 U.S. cents each at a street vendor, and the watermelon was about US$3.

Here only about 17 degrees north of the equator, the sun rises about this time every day and goes down again about 12 hours later. There's only a limited variation in the length of the day.

You sit on your screened porch with a view of the water. The weather is warm, as usual in the high 60s even early in the day. A refreshing breeze from the water eliminates the need for air-conditioning. The only time you turn on your small unit in your bedroom is in the summer, when there are still periods when the prevailing offshore breezes die down, sometimes for a couple of weeks at a time.

After breakfast, you putter around in your yard. Then you decide to go into town to buy some groceries and do your banking. You drive your gas golf cart (gas in 2006 reached near US$6 a gallon, but has fallen back a little) to the San Pedro Supermarket. It's about the size of a large convenience store in the U.S. You buy a pound of Mennonite cheese (US$4) and a bottle of One Barrel rum (US$9).

You decide to have lunch at an inexpensive local restaurant. The luncheon special of rice and beans is US$4.

After lunch, you come home and take a siesta. After watching a little cable TV, you and your partner decide to go out to dinner. You have your usual – grilled fish with rice, plus a Belikin or two. The total bill for two including 10% tax and 10% tip comes to US$24.

Tuesday
After breakfast, you take the water taxi to Belize City (US$20 round-trip) to take care of some business with your attorney.

You arrive at the Marine Terminal and decide to walk to your attorney's office on Albert Street. As usual, you get turned around in Belize City. It's not a big city, hardly more than an overgrown town, but the narrow streets lined with ramshackle buildings confusingly end up at canals and suddenly turn one-way. The city has a colorful street life, with people of all races and backgrounds jostling for space and sharing a word.

Finally you get to Albert Street. As you walk to the office, you're approached by a rail thin Creole who tries to sell you weed. "No man! Ah no need ganja tideh." You tell him you don't need any marijuana today, and he goes on his way. Since moving to Belize, you've picked up a little Creole — most everybody in Belize knows how to wap wa li Creole, or speak some Creole. You've also learned some Spanish.

After you finish your legal business, walking back to the Marine

Terminal, you see a tour bus full of pale-skinned, plump Americans, gawking at the street life of the city. A cruise ship must be in town. The Belize government, seeking the revenue from port charges, have encouraged the cruise companies to stop in Belize City. On some days, there are two or three ships in port at once, with thousands of day trippers tendered into the Tourist Village, built expressly for cruise industry. The harbor is too shallow to allow the big ships to dock.

After you get back home, you do some research on the internet. With your Belize Telecommunications Ltd. DSL service, you get decent surfing speed, but it's several times more expensive than back home. You pay around US$100 a month.

Unfortunately, the power goes out. Power on Ambergris Caye comes from Mexico, and occasionally — sometimes more than occasionally — there are blackouts. This time, the power is off for about three hours. There's no explanation of why it went out.

Wednesday
You decide to get in a little fishing today. So, early in the morning, you head out with a friend who has a small powerboat. After about two hours on the back side checking out bonefish spots for friend who is coming down and wants to try his luck with the bones, you make a stop in the fishing village of Sarteneja to check out a skiff a fellow there has for sale. Sarteneja boatbuilders are known all over Belize. Then you grab a cold Fanta. You spend a few hours trolling for snapper, and you also catch and release a couple of tarpon. Heading home, you make plans next week to go diving on the barrier reef west of San Pedro.

After a home-cooked dinner of conch ceviche and grilled snapper, you watch TV and retire early.

Thursday
Today, you decide to poke around the house, doing some repairs and piddling in your garden. Not everything grows well in the sandy, salty soil of the island, but by adding some black dirt you've had good luck with tomatoes, peppers, several kinds of squash including cho-cho, which your neighbors say looks like

the face of an old granny without teeth and all kinds of herbs including lemongrass and basil.

Friday

A lower molar is giving you a little problem, so you call a dentist you know in Chetumal, Mexico (though there are good dentists in Belize City, San Pedro and elsewhere), and his office says you can come in at 11 this morning. You hop the Tropic Air flight (US$47) from San Pedro to Corozal Town, then catch a bus (US$2) to cross the border. You take a taxi (US$3) from the ADO terminal to your dentist's office. The office is modern and clean and seems to have all the latest equipment. Your dentist says a filling has come out, and he replaces it. The cost? US$40.

Then you visit San Francisco, a large supermarket in Chetumal, where you pick up some antibiotics and other medicines for your partner. You don't need a prescription, and the total cost is less than one-half what you'd pay in the U.S. You have lunch at Los Cocos, where an expansive meal with good Mexican beers came to less than US$9.

Saturday

In the afternoon, you invite friends over for a cookout. The ground steak for hamburgers isn't as good as you'd like, but it's a successful party nonetheless. After the meal, you sit out on the deck, sip some rum and look at the waves breaking on the barrier reef a few hundred yards offshore.

Sunday

You go to English mass in at the Catholic Church on Barrier Reef Drive, and then go to BC's for the barbecue on the beach. Returning home, you read for a while, then snack on fresh fruit for Sunday supper, and go to bed early. You have to be rested and ready for another hard week in paradise.

GRADING AMBERGRIS CAYE FOR RETIREMENT, RELOCATION AND INVESTMENT

Ratings are on an A to F scale, just like your old high school report card. A is the top grade; F is failing. Grades are on a curve, relative compared to other areas in Belize.

Popularity with Expats	A
Safety	B
Overall Cost of Living	C-
Real Estate Costs	D
Investment Potential	B+
Leisure Activities	B+
Restaurants	A
Cultural Activities	D+
Infrastructure	C+
Business Potential	B+
Medical Care	C+
Shopping	C+

ADVANTAGES OF AMBERGRIS CAYE: • Largest expat community in Belize • Busy resort island atmosphere with the country's best   restaurants • Offers some of Belize's best beaches • Provides excellent water sports opportunities – diving, boating, fishing • No need for a car • Reasonably safe though burglaries are common

Real Estate on Ambergris Caye

Property prices on Ambergris Caye are among the highest in Belize. As elsewhere, prices vary tremendously depending on location and on the specific property. Houses and lots in predominantly Belizean areas, mostly on the back or lagoon side of the island, tend to be much less expensive than seafront property preferred by foreign investors and residents.   Demand in recent years generally has been strong for beachfront lots and beachfront homes. Appreciation has run 10 to 20% per year for many years, according to local real estate brokers, although this appreciation rate slowed in the 2001-2003 period, due to the economic slowdown in the United States, and stalled completely in 2008-2009, with the worldwide deep recession.

Agents point to beachfront property on North Ambergris, which went for US$450 a front foot in the late1980s that is offered for US$3,000 or more a front foot now.

Prices in Belize are to a great extent dependent on economic conditions in the United States and, to some extent, in Canada. When the U.S. sneezes, Belize catches cold.

Upfront taxes, especially on new condos and homes, can discourage middle-income buyers. With the 15% surcharge up front (5% stamp duty and 10% GST), buying a US$300,000 condo would entail an additional US$45,000 cash outlay upfront, although in some cases the GST and stamp duty is rolled into the offering price.

Condo development continues on the island. Some 700 new condo units have been constructed in the last several years, most on North Ambergris Caye.   A number of hotels have converted some or all of their units to "condotel" status. The idea is to sell now for immediate cash, then make 40 to 60% of revenues in management fees for running the hotel for absentee owners. Sales, however, have not always met expectations, as some investors are wary of condominium laws in Belize – condos are fairly new to Belize – and some have been burned by disputes with developers. Some developers offer limited financing, typically 20% down, with the balance payable over 10 years at around 12% interest. Usually, there's a balloon payment at the end of the term.

Timeshares have not fared well on Ambergris Caye or anywhere in Belize, though a number of condo hotels offer timeshares in a low-key way. Buyers have been few, and many who did buy quickly became dissatisfied with their purchase. The town council has passed regulations restricting activities of timeshare touts.

Building lots: Caribbean seafront building lots range from around US$3,000 to $6,000 per beachfront linear foot, and some are even higher. Less-expensive lots generally are on upper reaches of North Ambergris, which is accessible only by private boat or water taxi and has no electricity or other utilities. There you can find small beachfront lots from around US$50,000 and sometimes less; lots one row back from the beach from around US$20,000; and back lots from around US$10,000 to $15,000. Waterfront lots on the lagoon or backside of the island start at around US$500 per waterfront foot, with most under US$1,500 a foot. In general, lots a row back from the sea are just 30% of those directly on the water. Buyers should be aware that some beachfront lots have mangroves, not sand, on the waterside, and a permit is required to cut mangroves (though many mangroves have been illegally removed). Higher ground not subject to flooding obviously is more desirable, and more expensive, than low-lying property.

Homes: Two- or three-bedroom modern houses on the beach on North Ambergris Caye (access via water taxi or ferry) range from around US$200,000 (generally for a simple, wooden Belizean-style house) to well over US$1 million. Those south of San Pedro Town on the sea start at around US$250,000. Homes not on the water but with sea views are available from around US$100,000, but many run several hundred thousand dollars. At the top end, deluxe, recently built beachfront three and four bedroom homes may go for US$750,000 to $1,500,000 or more. Homes with "sunset views" – that is, on the west side or lagoon side of the island – start at around US$75,000 for a simple house.

Condos: Small one-bedroom condos without sea view start at around US$100,000, though most are US$125,000 or more. One-bedroom condos with sea views run about US$135,000 to $200,000. High-quality two- or three-bedroom condos with sea views range from around US$250,000 to $500,000 or higher. With the 10% GST on new condos, plus 5% transfer tax, and a surplus of inventory, the condo market in San Pedro and elsewhere has been hit hard, and some developers and owners are cutting prices.

Home construction: Building costs on Ambergris are relatively high, due to the need to dig deep foundations and install pilings for stability in the sandy soil, and to build with hurricane protection in mind. Bringing building supplies in by barge also adds to the cost. Expect to pay US$85-$175 or more a square foot for quality reinforced concrete construction. As elsewhere in Belize, labor costs are lower than in the U.S., but most building materials are more expensive. An exception is native hardwood lumber, which is beautiful and cheap.

PROPERTIES FOR SALE

Here are some sample listings offered by individuals and real estate companies in early 2010. Prices shown are asking prices. Due to issues of timeliness, we have not included the offering individual or real estate agent. Consider these as representative of property on the market at this time. For similar offerings go to the real estate websites listed in this book. Also, check out the new Ambergris Caye MLS, a local multiple listing service – www.mlsambergriscaye.com.

Beachfront lot with 200 ft. of sea frontage, Robles Point 14 miles north of San Pedro. US$330,000

Lagoon front lot in San Pablo area 1 1/2 miles south of San Pedro, 50 x 102 ft., with road access, electricity, telephone, municipal water and cable TV. Sunset views of San Pedro Lagoon. US$80,000

Beachfront lot with 75 ft. of sea frontage, 125 ft. deep, 7 miles north of San Pedro, annual taxes US$435, electricity to lot. US$279,000

Fourth row 100 x 100 ft. lot in Palm Bay, 22 miles north of San Pedro, US$18,000

Large commercial seafront parcel suitable for condo or resort development, 400 ft. beachfront x 600 ft. (approx. 5 1/2 acres), 8? miles north of San Pedro. US$1,800,000

Three-bedroom, three-bath 2,385 sq. ft. condo at Grand Caribe, 1 1/2 miles north of San Pedro, second floor unit with seaviews, use of three pools, marina. US$635,800

Two-bedroom, two-bath 1,275 sq. ft. furnished beachfront condo at Pelican Reef, 2 1/2 miles south of San Pedro, air-conditioning, all utilities including cable TV available, use of all hotel amenities including pool, pier. Annual property tax US$193. US$349,000

Two-bedroom, one-bath furnished 600 sq. ft. seafront condo at Banana Beach Resort 1 1/2 miles south of San Pedro, air-conditioning, all utilities including cable TV available, use of all hotel amenities including two pools, guaranteed rental income. US$145,000

One-bedroom, one-bath furnished 580 sq. ft. seafront condo at Mayan Princess, in San Pedro, ground floor, air-conditioning, all utilities including cable TV available. US$108,000

Beachfront three-bedroom, three and a half bath, 2,300 sq. ft. concrete house on 1/2-acre 9 miles north of San Pedro at Palmero Point. Reef and sea views from wrap around second-story veranda. Fully furnished. Separate one-bedroom caretaker's house. Total annual property tax US$128. US$798,000

Lagoon side two-bedroom, two-bath 1,250 sq. ft. home with water views, on 75 x 75 ft. lot in Tres Cocos area, 1 mile north of San Pedro. All utilities available. US$295,000

Small three-bedroom, one-bath government-built concrete house with lagoon view, on 50 x 75 ft. lot 1? miles south of San Pedro. Needs some repairs. US$57,000

Real Estate Developments
Here are selected new condo and real estate developments in Ambergris Caye. Most market primarily to foreign buyers.

Grand Baymen, www.grandbaymen.com. This condo development on 4 acres about 1/2 mile south of San Pedro focuses on moderately priced condos, not on the water. One-bedroom (720 sq. ft.) and two-bedroom (1,070 sq. ft) condos are priced from US$159,000 to $244,000. Financing is available for 10 to 15 years, at 11.5% for the first three years, and then U.S. prime rate plus 5.5%, with 50% down.

Grand Belizean Estates, tel. 501-226-2260; www.grandbelizeanestates.net. Grand Belizean Estates goes for the low end of the market, with lots starting at under US$8,000. It is located about 5 miles north of San Pedro. The development has 1,193 lots. Lots 60 x 75 ft. start at US$7,925 and the most expensive lots are US$13,000 US each. The developer claims 350 of the lots sold in the first 70 days. At this price, you don't get water views, paved roads or a clubhouse. In fact, currently there is no road at all to the development. The developer says electricity will be available "soon." Homes will have to have a septic tank system, and water likely will be sky juice. Property taxes are expected to be around US$25 a year.

Grand Caribe, 1 1/2 miles north of of the river channel, tel. 501-226-4726; www.grandcaribe.com. This high-quality upscale condominium development has 74 one-, two- and three-bedroom units in eight three- and four-story buildings in a horseshoe arrangement. It is on 5 acres with 500 ft. of beachfront. All units have sea views. There are three fresh-water swimming pools and a striking curved dock and pier. Rare in Belize, one of the buildings has elevator access to upper level condo units. Prices range from around US$395,000 to $715,000.

South Beach Belize, www.southbeachbelize.com. Developers of this controversial mega-project claim it will have condos, villas, hotels, a marina, casino, a theater, restaurants and retail space at the south end of the island, about 4 miles south of San Pedro. Everything will be done in an Art Deco style imitative of Miami's South Beach. Eventually, if it comes to fruition, the developer says it will be home to as many as 7,000 people. At present, nothing has been built.

San Pedro Real Estate Agents
Ambergris Seaside Real Estate, P.O. Box 163, San Pedro, Ambergris Caye, tel. 501-226-4545; www.ambergrisrealestate.com.

Casa Cayo Real Estate, Corner of Buccaneer and Pescador, San Pedro, tel. 501- 226-2791; www.casacayorealestate.net.

Diane Campbell, San Pedro, tel. 501-226-5203 or 610-5118; e-mail diane@dianecampbell.net.

Pelican Properties, San Pedro, tel. 501-226-3234; www.pelicanpropertiesbelize.com.

Southwind Properties, P.O. Box 1, San Pedro, Ambergris Caye, tel. 501-226-2005; www.belize-real-estate.net.

Sundancer Properties, Pescador Dr., San Pedro, tel. 501-226-4473; www.sundancerproperties.com.

Sunrise Realty, P.O. Box 236, #1 Barrier Reef Dr., San Pedro, Ambergris Caye; tel. 501-226-3737; www.SunriseBelize.com.

Triton Properties, Barrier Reef Dr., San Pedro; tel. 501-226-3783; www.triton-properties.com.

Short-Term Rentals on Ambergris Caye
The best way to find a rental house or apartment on Ambergris Caye is to come to the island and look around in person. The *San Pedro Sun* and *Ambergris Today* newspapers have a few rental classifieds, and AmbergrisCaye.com (www.ambergriscaye.com) has occasional rentals posted. Here are some sources of short-term house rentals:

Caye Management (Barrier Reef Drive, San Pedro, tel. 501-226-3077, www.cayemanagement.com) has many rental houses and condos on the island.

B-Lease (P.O. Box 184, San Pedro, tel. 501-226-2186, www.ambergriscaye.com/blease/) is a property management company that specializes in longer-term rentals of at least six months. Six-month rentals start at around US$400 per month and go up to over US$2,000 a month.

Three Palms Property Management, San Pedro; tel. 501-678-9977; www.threepalmsproperties.net. Handles mostly longer-term rentals (six months or more.)

Also consider short-term condo rentals. One good option is **Banana Beach** (P.O. Box 94, San Pedro, tel. 501-226-3890, fax 226-3891; www.bananabeach.com). Banana Beach has one-bedroom efficiencies from around US$900 a month plus utilities, or US$1,300 with utilities including air-conditioning. Other condo developments including **Paradise Villas** and **Royal Palm** may offer monthly rentals, especially in the off-season between Easter and early December.

GRADING CAYE CAULKER FOR RETIREMENT, RELOCATION AND INVESTMENT

Ratings are on an A to F scale, just like your old high school report card. A is the top grade; F is failing. Grades are relative compared to other areas in Belize.

Popularity with Expats	C+
Safety	B
Overall Cost of Living	B-
Real Estate Bargains	B-
Investment Potential	B+
Leisure Activities	C
Dining	B-
Cultural Activities	D-
Infrastructure	C-
Business Potential	C+
Medical Care	D+
Shopping	D-

ADVANTAGES OF CAYE CAULKER:
• Small, laid-back island atmosphere • Provides excellent opportunities for water activities – boating, fishing, diving
• Less expensive than San Pedro with opportunity for greater appreciation • No need for a car

Real Estate on Caye Caulker
Most of the development on

Caulker is concentrated in the one small village. Many families have long ties with the island and aren't interested in selling. Thus, the number of available properties is small. When properties do come on the market, the owners sometimes have an inflated idea of their value. One small budget hotel was offered in 2003 for US$3,500,000 – it remains for sale – for not much less than the total annual gross tourism revenue of the entire island!

Properties on Caye Caulker

Most of the real estate companies in San Pedro also have occasional listings on Caye Caulker. Here are some of the properties for sale on Caye Caulker in 2006, offered both by individuals and by real estate companies:

4 acres with 240 ft. of beachfront north of the Split. US$425,000

Seaside Cabanas, new hotel on the beach, with pool. US$2.3 million.

60 x 80 ft. lot, near airstrip. US$55,000

60 x 90 ft. lot, on sea, near airstrip. US$75,000

Three-bedroom, two-bath wooden house, fully furnished. US$125,000

OTHER CHOICE PLACES TO LIVE

Ambergris Caye is the most popular place for retirees and other expats to live in Belize, and Caye Caulker is growing in popularity, but there are many other choices.

Corozal in Northern Belize

Most visitors to Belize either never get to Corozal or pass through quickly en route somewhere else. But Corozal Town and nearby Consejo village offer a lot for those staying awhile: low prices, friendly people, a generally low-crime environment, the beautiful blue water of Corozal Bay and the extra plus of having Mexico next door for shopping. There's even a new Sam's Club in Chetumal, just across the border. Corozal is one of the undiscovered jewels of Belize. There's not a lot to do, but it's a great place to do it.

The Sugar Coast - sugarcane is a main agricultural crop here as it is in the adjoining Orange Walk district - is a place to slow down, relax and enjoy life. The climate is appealing, with less rain than almost anywhere else in Belize, and fishing is excellent. The sunny disposition of residents - Mestizos, Creoles, Maya, Chinese, East Indians and even North Americans - is infectious. Real estate costs in Corozal are among the lowest in Belize. Modern North American-style homes with three or four bedrooms in Corozal Town or Consejo Shores go for US$100,000 to around US$250,000, but Belizean-style homes start at less than US$35,000. Waterfront lots are available for US$75,000 or less, and big lots near the water are US$15,000-$30,000. Rentals are relatively inexpensive - US$200-$400 for a Belizean-style house or US$400-$1,000 for a modern American-style house.

Rural Orange Walk District in Northern Belize
Orange Walk Town - the name came from the orange groves in the area - could be any number of towns in Mexico. There's a formal plaza, and the town hall is called the Palacio Municipal. The businesses and houses along the main drag - Queen Victoria Avenue or the Belize-Corozal Road - have barred windows, and some of the hotels and bars are in fact brothels. In this setting, conservative Mennonites from Shipyard who come to town to sell produce look strangely out of place. However, Orange Walk Town is a gateway to a magical area of Belize - the wide sky, fertile land and unpeopled forests of Belize's northwest shoulder, pressed against the Guatemala border.

Cayo District in Western Belize
Cayo has a lot going for it: wide open spaces, cheap land, few bugs and friendly people. This might be the place to buy a few acres and grow oranges. The major towns are San Ignacio/Santa Elena, with a population of about 20,000, about 10 miles from the Guatemala border, and Belmopan City, the miniature capital of Belize, also with a combined population of around 20,000. Agriculture, ranching and, increasingly, tourism are the major industries here. About 30 years ago, the first small jungle lodges began operation around San Ignacio. Now

there is a flourishing mix of hotels, cottages and jungle lodges near San Ignacio and in the Mountain Pine Ridge, along with a lot of natural attractions and outdoor activities - canoeing, caving, hiking, horseback riding, to name a few. The country's most accessible Maya ruins are here, as well as Caracol, in its heyday a larger city-state than Tikal. Between Belize City and San Ignacio, Belmopan is the downsized capital of Belize, but the attractions are in the surrounding countryside. The Belize Zoo is nearby, as are several excellent jungle lodges. Along the scenic Hummingbird Highway are barely explored caves, wild rivers and national park areas. Small farms are available for US$25,000-$75,000.

Placencia on the Southern Coast

Placencia has the best beaches on the mainland, and it's an appealing seaside alternative to the bustle of Ambergris Caye. This peninsula in southern Belize has some 16 miles of beachfront along the Caribbean, a backside lagoon where manatees are frequently seen, two small villages, a few dozen hotels and restaurants and an increasing number of expatriates and foreign-owned homes. In recent years, the Placencia peninsula has been undergoing a boom, a boom that was slowed only temporarily by Hurricane Iris in 2001. Building lots by the score have been sold to foreigners who think they'd someday like to live by the sea. Beginning around 2004-2005, condo development on the peninsula took off, and now some 1,500 condos are either under construction or planned, though construction slowed down dramatically as the housing crunch and recession seized up markets in the U.S. and elsewhere. One condo project, the 60-unit Bella Maya north on the peninsula, shut down in early 2010, at least temporarily. Other projects have been put on hold.

Seafront real estate costs are higher in Placencia than anywhere else in Belize, except Ambergris Caye. Beachfront lots cost US$2,500 to $3,500 per front foot, making a seaside lot around US$100,000 or more. Lots on the lagoon or canal are less expensive. There is little North American-style housing available for sale or rent, and many expatriates are building their own homes, with building costs ranging upwards of US$100 per square foot, depending on type of construction. A contract to pave the peninsula road, a monster that everyone loves to hate, was signed in 2007, and as of this writing the road is paved from Placencia village to Maya Beach. It is expected to be completed by late 2010. A new airport is under construction just north of the peninsula. It is supposed to open in 2010, with limited international service. It's too early to say whether the international service will actually materialize.

Hopkins on the Southern Coast

On the southern coast of Belize in Stann Creek District between Dangriga and Placencia, Hopkins today is what Placencia was like just a decade or so ago. Expatriates are moving to Hopkins, a friendly Garifuna village that got telephones only in the mid-1990s, and to real estate developments nearby. New small seaside hotels and condo developments are going up in Hopkins and Sittee Point. Although at times the sand flies can eat you alive here, you can get in some excellent fishing and beach time, with day trips to the nearby Cockscomb jaguar reserve and boat trips to the reef. You'll love Hopkins if Placencia is too developed for you.

Punta Gorda in Southern Belize

Rainy, beautiful and remote, Punta Gorda in far southern Belize is the jumping-off point for unspoiled Maya villages and for onward travel to Guatemala and Honduras. Over the next few years as paving of the final 5-mile portion of the Southern Highway to Punta Gorda is completed and the road is extended into Guatemala, this area is expected to take off, both in terms of tourism and as a place for expatriate living. "PG," as it's known, is Toledo District's only population center, with about 5,500 people, mostly Garifuna, Maya and immigrants from Guatemala. Maya villages, hardly changed for centuries, are located around PG. Cayes and the south end of the barrier reef offer good snorkeling and fishing. Lumbering and fishing are about the only industries. Undeveloped land is inexpensive, with acreage beginning at a few hundred dollars an acre. Few North American-style homes are for sale. Quality rentals are fairly expensive due to demand from missionaries and lack of supply.

Private Islands

The days of buying your own private island for a song are long gone, but if you have money to burn and the willingness to rebuild after the next hurricane, one of Belize's remote islands could be yours, beginning at about US$100,000 and going up to several million. In 2005, Leo DiCaprio, the star of *Titantic,* bought Blackadore Caye, a 104-acre island near San Pedro, for a reported US$2.4 million, or about US$23,000 an acre.

Developers have been selling lots on a few small cayes. Keep in mind that transporting materials to the island, building there and maintaining the property likely will be much, much higher than on the mainland.

The beach in Placencia

WHAT THINGS COST IN BELIZE

Belize doesn't have a cost of living. It has several costs of living.

The traditional view is that Belize is the most expensive country in Central America, yet one of the least expensive in the Caribbean. While there's truth to that, it really doesn't take into account that the actual cost of living in Belize can vary from almost nothing to very high.

You can live in a luxury four-bedroom house, with air conditioning, telephones and faxes, a dishwasher, microwave and cable TV, U.S. food in your pantry and imported vodka in your glass, and you can spend thousands a month. Or you can live in a small Belizean-style house with no phone or internet, eat beans and rice and rice and beans, and drink local rum for US$300 a month or less. Most expats in Belize choose somewhere in between.

Some condos in Belize go for more than US$400,000, but one happy Belize resident built and equipped his small house, using his own labor, with thatch from nature and timbers from a lagoon, for US$4,000, and that includes furniture and kitchen equipment.

After all, per capita income in Belize is a fraction of that in the U.S. A weekly wage of US$125 to $150 for six days of work is considered pretty good. (But there are tour operators in San Pedro who make US$3,000 to $4,000 a month, so you can't generalize.) Tens of thousands of Belizeans live, and in many cases live comfortably, on a few thousand dollars a year. You can live like a Belizean, too. Or you can compromise, forsaking those high-cost icons of civilization such as 90,000 BTU air conditioners, while keeping the family car, boat or other toys that you enjoy. Live partly on the Belizean style, partly in the U.S. style, and enjoy the benefits of both, and you'll get more, perhaps for less.

One American expat, who returned to Colorado after living in Belize for five years, said he was surprised at how the cost of living in the U.S. had increased since he left. "Compared to Colorado Springs, ANYTHING in Belize is cheap. And I can't wait to get back — I just don't have enough money to live here in anything but poverty!"

Price Sampler

Here's a sampler of costs for common items in Belize, as of 2010. All prices are shown here in U.S. dollars. As in other countries, prices for many items vary depending on where and when you buy them.

Transportation

Gallon of regular unleaded gas: $4.65 (the pump price varies slightly by area, and fluctuates frequently reflecting the international price of oil - in 2008 and 2009 the price ranged from around US$2.50 to over $5)
Gallon of diesel fuel: $4.25
Bus fare from Belize City to San Ignacio: $2.50 regular, $3 express
Water taxi from Belize City to San Pedro, Ambergris Caye: $10
One-way adult airfare from Belize City municipal airport to Placencia: $84
One-way adult airfare from Belize City municipal airport to San Pedro: $35
Taxi fare within Belize City: $3-$5

Utilities/Telecommunications

1-kilowatt hour of current (electricity): $0.21
"Current" (electrical service) for 1000 KW monthly: $210
Installation of residential telephone: $50 plus $100 deposit ($500 if you are not a Belizean citizen or permanent resident)

Monthly charge for residential telephone: $10
10-minute call from Corozal to Belize City: $1
10-minute daytime call to U.S.: $8
DSL Internet access: $50 to $200 a month
Digital cellular service: $50 for 250 anytime minutes (incoming calls are free) plus 30 text messages
Water and sewer service: $10-$30+ (varies by area)
Butane, 100-pound tank, delivered: $47.50 (varies by area)
Bottled water, delivered: $2.50/gallon
"Dirt" (trash) pick-up: Free to $10 a month (varies by area)

Staples in Grocery Stores (Prices Vary by Store)
Red beans: $0.90 per pound
Coffee (Belizean, Gallon Jug): $8 per pound
Milk: $2.25 1/2 gallon
Ground steak (lean ground beef): $1.50 per pound
Pork chops: $2 per pound
Chicken: $1.25 per pound
Loaf of white bread: $1 (whole wheat $2.50-$3)
Corn tortillas, freshly made: $0.02-$0.04 each
Bananas: 10 to 20 for $1
Avocados (pears): 6 for $1 (varies seasonally)
Flour, bulk, 1 lb.: $1
Onions: $0.60 per pound (varies seasonally)
Soft drink, Coca-Cola, 12 oz.: $0.50 - 0.75 each
Local rum, liter: $7 - $12
Sugar: $0.27 per pound
Crackers (Premium Saltines): $3.32
Cigarettes, Independence local brand: $3 a pack
Canned soup (Campbell's Chicken Noodle): $1.80
Cereal (Raisin Bran): $5
Cooking oil (1-2-3 brand from Mexico), 1/2 liter: $1.75

Household Items
Mennonite-made wood dining table: $175
Music CD (pirated): $5
Whirlpool 12,000 BTU air-conditioner: $700
Panasonic 1350-watt microwave: $165
Mabe (Mexican) frost-free 16 cubic foot refridgerator: $675
Small home appliances at Mirab, Courts, Brodies, Hofius or other stores: about 25% to 50% more than prices in the U.S.

Entertainment
Fish and beans and rice at local restaurant, Hopkins: $4
Fish, French fries and cole slaw dinner, San Pedro: $12
Lobster dinner at nice restaurant, Belize City: $30
Movie theater ticket, Princess, Belize City: $8.50
Rum drink at bar, Placencia: $2.50-$3
Belikin beer at bar in Cayo: $2-$2.50

Shelter Costs
Rent for simple two-bedroom house in Corozal Town: $200 to
$400

Rent for modern two-bedroom apartment in San Pedro: $800 to $1,800

Cost to build a reinforced concrete home: $40 to $100 per sq. ft., finished out moderately

Small concrete house and lot in Belmopan or Cayo: $30,000 to $100,000

Modern three-bedroom house and beachview lot in Consejo: $145,000--$250,000

Two-bedroom condo on Ambergris Caye: $200,000 to $750,000

Medical Care
Office visit, private physician: $25
Teeth cleaning, private dentist: $40
Root canal and crown, private dentist: $250 - $500

Building Supplies
50# bag of cement: $6 to $7
"Prefab" Mennonite House, 800 sq. ft, set up on your lot, $16,000+

Family Budgets on the Islands

As noted, the cost of living varies greatly in Belize, depending on your lifestyle, preferences and place of residence. Here are a couple of sample budgets.

Monthly Budget (in U.S. Dollars) for Affluent Couple in San Pedro

This budget reflects the cost of living for a 45-year-old affluent expat who rent a two-bedroom condo on Ambergris Caye. Assumption: The couple owns a golf cart, owns a small boat and spends freely for entertainment and personal expenses. They have major medical insurance with an international firm. It also assumes the couple has income from outside Belize that is not taxed in Belize.

Rent	$1,250
Electricity (1500 KW)	315
Telephone (including long distance)	150
Water	100
Bottled water	80
Butane	70

Groceries	400
DSL internet	100
Entertainment and dining out	550
Cable TV	25
Golf cart maintenance, gas and upkeep	75
Boat expenses	200
Health insurance	300
Out-of-pocket medical/dental care	150
Flights to Belize City (twice monthly)	260
Other travel expenses	200
Clothing	100
Household help (part-time)	250
Other personal expenses	200
Total	**US$4,775**

Monthly Budget (in U.S. Dollars) for Middle-Class Couple on Caye Caulker

This budget reflects the cost of living for a 55-year-old expat couple who own their own small house on Caye Caulker. It assumes that the couple has paid for their US$150,000 house and therefore do not have a house payment. Also assumed: they have a couple of bicycles and they choose to purchase major medical health insurance from an international insurer, and that the couple has income from outside Belize that is not taxed in Belize.

Electricity (750KW a month)	US$158
Telephone (including long distance)	100
Butane	50
Groceries	250
Cable TV	40
Internet	50
Entertainment and dining out	200
Property tax	25
Health insurance	300
Water taxis to Belize City	60
Out-of-pocket medical expenses	150
Home insurance (at 1.5% of value)	185
Clothing	75
Other personal expenses	100

Household help/care taker (limited part-time)	100
Other	95
Total	**US$1,938**

GETTING ALONG IN BELIZE

If you're looking for a place to live or to retire that's just like back home, only better, for a United States or a Canada on the cheap, for Florida with ruins, reefs and rum, you may get a rude awakening when you move to Belize.

Because Belize just isn't like the USA. Or Canada. It does have cheap rum, awe-inspiring ruins, beautiful Caribbean seas, and much more.

But the rules are different. The people who make and enforce the rules are different. Sometimes there are no rules. Sometimes there is a set of rules for you, and a different one for everyone else. Just about every expat resident of Belize has some story to tell about problems he or she faced in adjusting to life in Belize - or, in not adjusting. Let's look at some of the differences, and what they mean to you as a potential resident or retiree.

Population of a Small City

First, Belize is a country with a population hardly bigger than a small city in the U.S. Even including recent immigrants from El Salvador, Guatemala and Honduras, the population of the entire country is only around 333,000.

Imagine the difficulties your hometown would have if it suddenly became a country. Belize has to maintain embassies, establish social, educational and medical systems, raise a little army, and conduct affairs of state and international diplomacy, all with the resources of a small city.

You can see the difficulties Belize faces in just getting by in a world of mega states. It lacks the people resources, not to mention the tax base and financial resources, to get things done in the way North Americans expect. If you're a snap-to-it, get-it-done-right kind of person, you're going to wrestle with a lot of crocodiles in Belize.

No More Power
Most people seeking retirement or residency in Belize are white middle-class North Americans, from a society still run by white middle-class North Americans.

Belize, on the other hand, is a truly multi-cultural society, with Creoles, Mestizos, Maya, Garifuna, Asians, and what in the rest of Latin America would be called Gringos, living together in complex and changing relationships, living together in probably more harmony than anyone has a right to expect. In several areas, Creoles dominate; increasingly, in other areas Spanish-speaking Belizeans and immigrants dominate.

One thing is for certain, though: In this mix, North Americans, Europeans and Asians have very limited power.

Money talks in Belize, of course, as it does everywhere. Most of Belize's tourism industry is owned by foreign interests. Much of its industry and agriculture is controlled by multinational companies. Politically, however, the typical North American resident of Belize is powerless. He or she has no vote and is truly outside the political process.

That's the fate of expats everywhere, but some who come to Belize, seeing a country that is superficially much like back home, are shocked that they no longer have a power base and are, in a political sense at least, truly powerless.

The North American or European is not so much at the bottom rung of Belizean society, as off the ladder completely. If you like to pick up the phone and give your congressional representative a piece of your mind, you're going to miss this opportunity in Belize.

Culture Shock
Culture shock is what happens when everything looks about 20 degrees off kilter, when all the ways you learned were the right ways to deal with people turn out to be wrong. It is a state, someone said, of temporary madness.

Usually it happens after about six to 18 months in a new situation. At first, you're excited and thrilled by the new things you're seeing. Then, one day, you just can't stand one more dish of stewed chicken. In Belize, culture shock is sometimes masked by the surface familiarity. Most Belizeans speak English, albeit a different English. They watch - such a shame - American television. They drive American or Japanese cars. They even accept U.S. currency.

But, underneath the surface sameness, Belize is different, a collection of differences. Cases in point: The ancient Mayan view of time, cyclical and recurring, and even the Mayan view today, are grossly different from the linear way urban North Americans view time. The emerging Hispanic majority in Belize has social, religious and political views that are quite different from the views of the average North American, or, even of the typical Belizean Creole. A Belize Creole saying is "If crab no walk 'e get fat, if 'e walk too much 'e lose claw." Is that a cultural concept your community shares?

In many cases, family connections and relationships are more important in Belize than they are in the U.S. or Canada. Time is less important. Not wanting to disappoint, Belizeans may say "maybe" when "no" would be more accurate. Otherwise honest men may take money under the table for getting things moving. Values North Americans take for granted, such as "work hard and get ahead," may not apply in Belize in the same way. Physical labor, especially agricultural work and service work, because of the heritage of slavery and colonialism, is sometimes viewed as demeaning among some Belize groups. A Belizean may work long hours for himself - fishing or logging can be backbreaking labor - but be reluctant to do so for an employer.

Respect, Not Money
Respect is important in Belize. If you make a pass at a friend's girl, you may end up on the wrong end of a knife or machete. If you diss one of your employees or neighbors, you may find yourself in a bad situation on a dark night. Just when you least expect it, you may get jumped on a back street and beat nearly to death. If you say something bad about a politician or a business owner, it may come back and bite you years later.

Belizeans have long memories, and they don't take well to criticism, especially not from outsiders.

On the other hand, Belizeans can be surprisingly rough and tumble in their personal relationships. They'll say the nastiest things to each other, just run the other guy down for being stupid and a total fool, and then the next day both parties forget about it and act like they've been friends or cousins all their lives, which they have been.

The best advice is to make as many friends in Belize as you can. Sooner or later, you'll need them.

No Wal-Marts in Belize

Belize has no Wal-Marts. No K-Marts. No Home Depots. No Circuit Cities. No McDonald's restaurants.

While this lack of homogenization is in Belize's favor, it also means that you can't go down to your neighborhood hyperstore and select from 40 kinds of dish soap, or 18 brands of underwear. Rum may be US$7 a bottle, but Cheetos may be US$5 a bag. Every CD player, nearly every piece of plumbing and electrical equipment, every car and truck, every pair of scissors, every bottle of aspirin, is imported, and often transshipped thousands of miles from one port to another before it gets to the final destination in Belize. Then it's carried on a bus or under a Cessna seat somewhere else.

Some items simply aren't available in Belize, or supplies may be spotty. Bags of cement, for example, sometimes are in short supply, and the cost, around US$8 to $9 for a 50-pound bag, is higher than you'd pay back home. To get ordinary items such as building nails or a certain kind of auto part, you may have to call several different suppliers. It may take a full day to run down a few construction items you need.

Belize's small population is spread out over a relatively large area, served by a network of bad roads (though they are getting better), old planes and leaky boats. Although the government is shifting its focus from excise and import taxes more to consumption taxes such as the new Goods and Services Tax, much of government revenue still comes from import taxes, so the prices you pay may reflect a tax of 20 to 80% or more.

In short, Belize is an inefficient market of low-paid consumers, a country of middlemen and mom 'n pop stores, few of which could last more than a month or two in a highly competitive marketplace like the U.S.

This is what gives Belize its unique flavor in an age of franchised sameness. But, you better Belize it, it also provides a lot of frustration and higher prices.

About LAN SLUDER

Lan Sluder has been banging around Belize for almost 20 years. He is the founder and editor of *Belize First Magazine,* now an online magazine, *BelizeFirst.com,* and is the author of several books on Belize, including *Fodor's Belize (2010)*, *Living Abroad in Belize* (2005), *Belize First Guide to Mainland Belize* (2001), *Adapter Kit: Belize* (2001), *Easy Belize* (2010), *San Pedro Cool* (2002, revised and released as an eBook, 2007) and *Belize Islands Guide* (2010). A former newspaper editor in New Orleans, Sluder also has done a Frommer's guidebook to the coast of the Carolinas and Georgia, a Fodor's guide to the Great Smoky Mountains National Park, co-authored several other books and has contributed articles to many magazines and newspapers including *Caribbean Travel & Life, New York Times, Chicago Tribune, Miami Herald, St. Petersburg Times, Bangkok Post, Tico Times, Globe & Mail* and *Where to Retire.* You can reach him at lansluder@gmail.com.